LIFEGUARD BLOOD: *Four Brothers Share Their Harrowing Stories From The Beach*

David Wagner

ISBN: 1546438874
ISBN-13: 978-1546438878

PREFACE

"A family is a place where minds come in contact with each other." ~ Buddha

Summer of 1952, Chicago, Illinois

The crowd had begun to swarm the two lifeguards carrying the unresponsive body of an eight-year-old girl out of the water, and up to the hot, wet sand of the beach. Billy Wagner was tense, with sweat dripping off the tip of his nose as he fumbled around trying to assemble the ventilator. Nobody had witnessed this girl drowning; she'd been found floating in chest-deep water. Billy was one of only two young men who might save her now, through administering CPR.

A heavyset Chicago police sergeant was doing the best he could to give the two rescuers the space they needed to work, extending his arms in front of the hovering crowd of onlookers. His black uniform contrasted noticeably with his pale Irish complexion, now pink with sunburn. "Alright, step back! Step back, why don't you? Let them do their jobs!" After he'd managed to herd them back a few feet, he looked down to see how the rescuers were managing.

The officer's eyes instantly widened in stark horror. The little girl on the ground, now dead, was his own daughter!

In dazed disbelief, Billy took in the traumatic scene before him of the other officers trying to console their sergeant. He had done everything in his power to bring this beautiful little girl back to life, but the physician had pronounced her dead 20 minutes later. This was Rainbow Beach in Chicago, one of the busiest beaches on all the Great Lakes, and the place lifeguard Billy Wagner would learn brutal lessons about life and death.

Swimming hadn't always been a big part of Billy's life. At eight years old, he'd been pushed into a public swimming pool by an older bully. Unable to swim at the time, he would have drowned if he hadn't been able to scratch his way back to the pool wall. He spent all that night coughing up water that had entered his lungs. After this, he vowed to himself that he would learn how to swim, which he accomplished without even one formal lesson. He took it upon himself to walk six blocks everyday to the neighborhood YMCA. The first ten minutes or so he would just watch the more experienced swimmers until he built up enough courage to give it a try. He would always enter the shallow corner of the pool, and his first attempt would be a doggie paddle style swim from one side of the corner to the next. Eventually as he gained confidence he would put his face in the water, blow his bubbles and attempt swimming the crawl. The distance from wall to wall would progressively get longer.

As a teenager, he read about the Chicago Times Swim Meet and decided to catch the city bus across town to compete in it. He finished the competition victoriously, winning all the events he had entered. When he returned home, however, he was greeted by an angry father who was sore at him for not painting the garage that day. Billy told his dad about winning the meet, but his father had just smiled and said, "You can paint the garage next Saturday."

As a high school sophomore, Billy became a beach lifeguard for the city of Chicago. The water of Lake Michigan can get very rough, and the frequent crowds flocking in from all over Chicago make it a challenging place to work. At age 20, Billy was promoted to captain, and although he turned it down at first, finally becoming lifeguard captain was one of the best experiences he would ever have.

One summer's day, on a private beach just north of Rainbow Beach, the body of a middle-aged man floated in. Billy, now Captain Wagner, and his first mate responded. When they arrived on the scene, the victim was clinically dead. They decided they should both work on the man for practice…after all, the first mate was in medical school. So, switching back and forth between them, they did ventilations and compressions for a half-hour. When the firemen showed up, they watched the two lifeguards, and told them to continue what they were doing. An hour later, a physician showed up to officially pronounce the victim dead. To the doctor's shock, however, he detected a faint pulse! The man was later brought to the hospital, and within a couple of weeks made a full recovery. It felt wonderful to the young lifeguard captain, after his earlier trauma with the eight-year-old child dying under his care, to get the upper hand on death this time.

Bill continued his swimming career at the University of Utah, where he was the recipient of a full scholarship. He often felt isolated, though, because most of his teammates were Mormon. Insecure and not certain he belonged there, he talked to his father, who encouraged him to give it a chance, and to challenge the swim team captain to a race. Bill wound up winning. During his swimming career, he achieved status as team captain, an All-Conference Champion, and holding records in the butterfly, and individual medley.

With so much of his success inspired by others, Bill knew he wanted to teach and coach. In 1955, he received a Bachelor's of Science in Physical Education, followed by his Master of Science in Education in 1956, for which his thesis was an evaluation of high school swim programs throughout Utah. Interestingly, he discovered that despite having regulation-sized pools, many high school programs were inadequate. After rating each school in his study, he disseminated his findings. To his satisfaction, it appeared that his report served as impetus for improvements made to some of the schools' programs.

Bill was drafted into the United States Army, and served dutifully for two years. While in the service, he was invited to play on the All-Army and All-Armed Forces swimming, and water polo teams. This was a memorable time for him, because it afforded him the opportunity to tour and compete against other NATO countries.

After serving in the army, he went to San Diego in search of a teaching position. In 1959, he obtained a position at Oceanside High School, where he remained for 12 years. In 1960, he started the boy's swim team, which according to him, consisted mainly of surfers who had little or no competitive swimming experience. By 1963, Bill's swim team began a streak of successes, achieving nine consecutive league titles, and two back-to-back California Interscholastic Federation (CIF) titles. Bill was also honored as CIF Coach of the Year.

In April of 1964, he married the love of his life, Ruth. They say opposites attract…Ruth was a dancer and gymnast, with a petite, well-defined figure. Standing next to the 6'3" tall and 190-pound swimmer was a complete contrast, but it suited both of them just fine. Ruth had graduated cum laude from the University of Arizona with a double major in psychology and liberal arts. Born in Montana on Fort Belknap Indian Reservation where her dad, Dr. Paul J. Pauliny, was in charge of the hospital. He immigrated from Czechoslovakia after receiving his medical degree from the University of Prague. It always impressed Ruth that her father spoke seven languages. Later, they moved to Tucson Arizona, where he worked for the San Xavier Sanatorium as Superintendent and Physician. Ruth was four years old when her dad died of Bright's disease, which was supposedly linked to Strep throat that he had as a child.

Heartbroken, her mother Edith was left to raise Ruth and her older sister Beth by herself. They moved back to New Jersey to be with relatives. Nothing seemed to give her solace. Inconsolable, Edith decided to move back to Tucson where her daughters would be raised. As young adults, the young women, and their mother would move to Vista, California of all places. Ruth found a job teaching at an elementary school. Bill and Ruth met on a blind date set up by mutual friends, and married within a year. Nobody could ever fill Paul's shoes, Edith idolized him. Ultimately, Edith died of a broken heart, right before the birth of Bill and Ruth's first child.

Ruth had always wanted a big family, full of boys, and she got exactly that. By 1971, their family had grown to include five children: Mike, the oldest; followed by Lori, the only girl; Scott, the middle child; and lastly, twins David and Neal. The parenting philosophy of Bill and Ruth was to "keep them all hungry and tired" to minimize the chaos. Two blocks away from the family home was Brooks Street Pool, and every day the young kids would ride their bikes there, and swim for an hour-and-a-half.

Lori had it tough being the only girl in the family, but out of all the Wagner kids, she was by far the most disciplined. She ultimately focused most of her time and energy on education, and graduated Oceanside High School as the salutatorian. She eventually went to Northwestern Medical School, and became a pediatrician. It was also a blessing for Ruth to have a girl because it allowed both of them to share that special mother/daughter bond. As Ruth reflected on the realization that her daughter was now a physician like her father, she could hear her mother's famous words, "Your father would be so proud."

Some of the biggest fights in the household were over the last piece of pizza or chicken in the box. Ruth was definitely the brains and organizer behind the elaborate operation of feeding five active kids. The amount of milk consumed each week was equivalent to what a small army might put away. Thank goodness for Price Club (later Costco) stores! The family rarely went out to eat; it was a special occasion just to go to McDonald's. They were all lean, and very scrappy.

The biggest rules—besides to not destroy the house or each other—were that they would all eat dinner together every night, and any fights had to be settled before going to bed. The boys would constantly fight, and there was an unwritten rule against any punching in the face. When out in public, however, the kids were very protective of one another.

Dinner was the only time of day that everyone was sitting down all together to reconnect after a hectic day. Everyone knew that mom is home cooking so you better be back by 6:30 or shit would hit the fan! It was a time of drama and learning. It started off with a prayer. Since there are seven of us total, each family member had a day of the week to say grace. The boys would try to outdo each other by seeing who could be the most like our minister who could be corny at times. Usually, when someone tried to be overtly philosophical the snickering and snorting would begin. The more we tried to control ourselves the more we exploded with laughter. Especially when Scott started his obnoxious, contagious giggle. No one wanted to be by dad when this started because of his intense authoritarian presence. His scowl meant you were seconds away from being physically removed from the dinner table.

One time, Mike got in trouble, and Bill became angry, so Ruth tried to divert him by saying, "Guess what happened with Scott at school today?" Bill then proceeded to smack Scott in the head. "Honey, he got an 'A' on his spelling test!" Ruth protested. Bill grumbled, "Well, I'm sure he did *something* bad." The rest of the kids laughed under their breath, not wanting to be next.

The Wagner clan learned a lot of vocabulary words just by listening to their parents talk—words such as facetious, tenacious, and integrity. They learned about current events, politics, and geography. Bill shared the importance of compassion, always saying, "Don't hit someone when they are down." Other ideas relayed were to pull for the underdog, and that being the "Cinderella Story" makes sports more exciting. To be sure, dinner time at the Wagner house always came with some useful information, or at least an entertaining show!

After years of swimming, surfing, and being Junior Lifeguards, all five kids would lifeguard for the city of Oceanside. In 1987, the Wagner family comprised 10% of the city's entire lifeguard staff!

ACKNOWLEDGMENTS

To my wife Jennifer, children Cole and Brianna, thank you for your love and support.

To my parents and siblings, thank you for sharing your stories.

To my friend Janice Grodsky, thank you for making this book a reality.

TABLE OF CONTENTS

CHAPTER 1

BECOMING A LIFEGUARD

"Believe you can, and you're halfway there." ~ Teddy Roosevelt

Turning 16 years old back in 1987 meant going down to the Department of Motor Vehicles, and getting your driver's license. This was, of course, a highly-anticipated rite of passage, separating those with freedom from those with none. Failing the written exam or the driving test was not an option, as the result was unspeakable harassment from brothers and friends alike. Worse, it would render me, or any other unfortunate test-taker ineligible for lifeguard try-outs. Luckily, my newly acquired driver's license took its place in my wallet alongside my American Red Cross First Aid and CPR cards. Now, all I had to do was show up on the first Saturday of spring break, in late March, and run the gauntlet of all the grueling tests required for me to earn my spot as a City of Oceanside Lifeguard. Because lifeguarding had already become a family tradition in the Wagner household, expectations from the people closest to me were particularly high.

The month of March in Southern California typically brings the coldest annual ocean water temperatures, averaging in the mid-50's. Of course, this is the same month for all this region's lifeguarding agency tryouts. Candidates in Hawaii or Florida are a bit more blessed, as the ability to adapt to, and perform in extreme cold is not a factor in their selection process. To acclimate ourselves to the chill, my twin brother Neal and I would swim behind our older brother Scott on a paddle-board twice a week for a month. Managing coldness is one of the biggest contributors to making it or breaking it in lifeguard work. Even swimmers who are the strongest or fastest fail despite their ability if they cannot perform in adverse conditions. The best prospective lifeguards are those who have spent a substantial amount of time in both the pool and ocean. Time in the pool builds speed and endurance, but ocean experience is necessary for all the other needed skills, including a healthy respect for the natural elements.

Diving into icy water takes your breath away, and makes your heart race—an instant, and guaranteed adrenaline rush. Initially, the lungs overcompensate by hyperventilating, i.e. "rabbit breathing", and this can only be overcome by consciously forcing yourself to control your breathing through focusing on exhaling all the air in your lungs before taking the next breath. This is an adaptive skill mastered only through actual exposure and practice.

The morning of the try-outs, Neal and I ate nothing. We were beyond nervous as we climbed into our first car, a 1966 Buick Wildcat, and headed down the road to Brooks Street Pool. Here we would be evaluated for the first set of skills before finishing up at the beach. Looking around the deck, we noticed collegiate swimmers wearing parkas with the names of their respective schools on the back. The minimum age for employment was 16 years old, and we were surrounded by older, bigger, and far less nervous hopefuls. In all, there were about 40 applicants vying for eight available spots.

After introductions, they gave us all pencils, and a 50-question multiple choice test on First Aid, CPR, and general lifeguarding practices. To go on to the next phase of the try-outs, we had to score 80%. I gave the test my attention, but had to battle all the dread-filled thoughts in my head about how tough this day was going to be. Even though I was nervous, I passed with an 88%. Next was the pool swim, during which we had to swim 600 yards in under 10 minutes. This was the easiest part of the day, and I cruised in with a final time of 7:55.

Before I knew it, it was time for our two ocean swims. Right before we headed down to the beach, someone remarked, "The surf is pumping!" I groaned inwardly. Surrounded by the smell of chlorine mingled with decomposing seaweed and salt air, we made our way towards the sand on the south side of Oceanside Pier. Our group of anxious wannabes huddled in front of the lifeguard headquarters, and as I gazed out on the water, I noticed large, orange buoys floating hundreds of yards past the breaking, six-foot surf. *That is my mission*, I breathed silently. *Get around those as fast as I can.*

As the lifeguard captain, Matt Stephens, gave us final instructions about the next phase of testing, I suppressed the urge to puke. "We are now going to do a run-swim-run," he barked. "You are going to run a quarter-of-a-mile down the beach, and make a left-shoulder turn around the red flag. Once you come back, you will left-shoulder-turn around the red flag at our current location. Then you will swim out to the large orange buoys, and go around both of them counterclockwise. Once you return to shore, you will repeat the run. This has to be done in less than 27 minutes," he concluded. The swim was approximately 1000 yards.

We were like zombies, filing down to the starting line in silence. My head had a lot to say, though. *This is it. If I don't do well, I will be the only boy in the family not to become a beach lifeguard.* Neal looked just as nervous, his face pasty with a haunted expression.

Cutting through my thoughts, the air horn blasted loudly. *Stay with Neal*, came my instinct. *Power of the pack!* The initial run seemed like a blur, my mind on auto-pilot, my legs pure adrenaline as I raced for the icy water.

My running morphed into a high-knee gallop as I hit the water, and made my way through the shallows. When the water reached my waist, it was time for me to dolphin under the waves. With my arms in a streamlined stretch above my head, I took a deep breath and dove. Immediately, the air was forced out of my lungs as I screamed primitively under the water. Fight or flight kicked in as my nervousness became determination. *I will win cold water! You've got nothing on me cold water! You've got this Wags!* Then, I lowered my head, and began to crank it out!

As my frigid body became numb, I concentrated on exhaling my air and blowing bubbles, helping me calm my quick, shallow breathing response to the cold water. Soon, my strokes became slower, broader, and rhythmic. The first buoy was in front of me before I knew it. *You're doing great,* I told myself. *Keep it up!* Once I rounded the second buoy, I had to look up to ensure my course to the beach was as straight as possible. Every ten strokes or so, I popped my head up to reorient myself to the most direct path. Navigating long open-water swims can be confusing, but the glassy water, and smell of bait fish not too far off were strangely comforting to me.

As I neared the beach, I became more aware of the swells coming in. I wanted to harness their energy to ease my workload. A wave can be like a beach taxi or free-ride—all you have to do is hold your breath and catch it. No such luck today, though. *Typical,* I thought irritably. *On the way out, I get hit by waves, and on the way in, there's a lull in the surf.* By the time a set of waves came rolling in, I was too far on the inside, and the waves were just breaking on top of me in the impact zone. The crashing waves put me through the "rinse cycle," throwing me around like a rag-doll, churning up the water, and making swimming difficult. I was gasping for air, and fatigue was setting in, but at least I was being propelled towards shore.

After the big breakers had their way with me, I caught a smaller inshore wave that put me into waist-deep water. It was time again to run. The blood that had been pumping through my shoulders and back was now needed in my legs...no easy task after being in the cold for so long, and the most difficult transition of any run-swim-run at this time of year in Oceanside. My body felt tight, heavy, and unresponsive from the numbing water, but I sprinted up the beach with everything I had left. Looking down the beach I saw two competitors between Neal and myself about forty yards away. With a half mile run left, it now became my mission to close the gap. I felt stiff like the tin man after the rain storm on the Wizard of OZ, but I had to open up my stride. My mind knew what needed to be done and went into a meditative state while making further demands on my body. After rounding the southern flag I passed one person and had 10 yards to overcome the next. Surprisingly, I did this within twenty seconds. Now I basically paced and drafted off Neal. He, more or less guided us in to the finish. *I better of made the time,* I thought. I stood doubled over trying to catch my breath with Neal. Our older brothers Mike and Scott came over and patted us on the back, telling us we made the time and did a hell of a job.

It wasn't over yet, though. After getting ten minutes to rest and warm up, it would be time for the sprint swim. It was a race through the surf, past the waves, and back to shore in the fastest time. At this point in our lives, Neal and I were tall and skinny, and it was seemingly impossible for us to gain weight no matter how much we ate. Going into survival mode, we headed to the lifeguard station parking lot and lay face down on the warm concrete. We resembled washed-up seal pups, but didn't care. "All we have to do is sprint in and out of the surf, and we are golden," Neal said. He was trying to be encouraging, but he sounded like a stroke patient...he was shivering so badly, he couldn't pronounce all the syllables of his words. "Yep," I replied, too tired to pick up my head as drool streamed from my mouth into a little pool on the pavement.

In the end, the sprint swim turned out to be very validating and boosted our waning confidence. The surf was sizable, and many of the pool swimmers didn't know how to navigate this part of the testing like we did. As experienced ocean swimmers and surfers, Neal and I took full advantage of all the time we'd spent in the surf. We entered the water well south of the other candidates because of the current. We knew the key to winning this race was catching a wave on the way back in. Succeeding here was about timing and using all available resources. We caught our wave and easily finished in the top five.

After the physical part of the testing was over, we had to perform CPR on a manikin and be scored on our technique. Years of being Junior Lifeguards plus having older brothers who were lifeguards helped Neal and I to ace this portion of the test. Fourteen of us remained out of the initial approximately 40 applicants, and we were all given interview appointments to take place at city hall later that afternoon.

I wore an ill-fitting, hand-me-down suit for my first "big boy" interview. I wasn't nervous because the interview seemed like nothing after surviving the brutality of the morning events. The point of the interview was to see what kind of human being I was, and I had no reservations about showing them. Looking back, I really had no clue about social graces, but one thing I did have was a whole lot of arrogance, which I suppose isn't terribly unusual in a 16-year-old boy. My swim coach, tenth grade history teacher, and a family friend had all written letters of recommendation. I was feeling invincible and full of myself, two qualities I now know were not in my favor.

"Congratulations getting this far!" the captain said, as he introduced the interview panel, which consisted of a lieutenant, the lifeguard chief, and the city's human resources representative, there to make sure everyone was playing legal and fair. It amazed me that the chief didn't look like a lifeguard or even suited for such a lofty title. He seemed out of place given the physical prowess of all the other men in the room. There was no way he could do any part of the job of a lifeguard on a physical level—in my youthful ignorance, I had no idea of the political inner workings of such a large agency.

Neal and I were both offered positions that summer. An accomplishment that shaped our future careers and the rest of our lives, just as it did for our two older brothers Scott and Mike. In late May, we started lifeguard training and by June were in uniform and becoming men on the sands of Oceanside's beaches.

DAVID WAGNER

CHAPTER 2

MIKE THE TRAILBLAZER

"I really don't know why it is that all of us are committed to the sea, except I think it's because in addition to the fact that the sea changes, and the light changes, and ships change, it's because we all come from the sea. And it is an interesting fact that all of us have in our veins the exact same percentage of salt in our blood that exists in the ocean, and, therefore, we have salt in our blood, in our sweat, in our tears. We are tied to the ocean. And when we go back to the ocean we are going back from wherever we came."
~ John F. Kennedy

Mike is "everyone's favorite Wagner." He is the oldest sibling and probably the most approachable and engaging. He has a witty sense of humor. At 6' and 185 pounds he is the smallest of all the boys, but he is a scrapper and by far the sorest loser!

The following is Mike's story:

At the age of eight, my mom and dad took me to a meeting that would change the rest of my life completely. It was the kick-off for a new summer program in the city of Carlsbad, California called Junior Lifeguards. My dad had mentioned that a couple of his former students were heading up the program, and I knew right from the start I wasn't going to have a choice in whether I joined. My parents' childrearing philosophy was to keep us kids busy, tired, and out of trouble. So, along with 20 to 30 other kids, most or all of them older than me, I listened to the leaders describe what would be involved, the hours, and how long the program would last. Water safety, first aid, lifesaving skills, and a lot of physical conditioning were among the parts of being a Junior Lifeguard. I was not excited. It sounded like a lot of work, and I didn't know anyone else doing it.

Not having any older brothers or sisters, I was also used to being the guinea pig for my parents' ideas about wholesome activities for kids. In two weeks, I was informed, there would be tryouts which would include swimming, holding your breath underwater, and treading water. These basic skills are, in fact, still used today to test potential Junior Lifeguards (JG's). There were two reasons why I knew I wouldn't have a problem with the tryout: 1) Due to his background in swimming and lifeguarding, my dad had put me in the water when I was knee-high to a newt, and I was swimming every day, and 2) If I did fail the test, my dad would want me to get back in the water until I *did* pass!

Like riding a bike, or your first day of school, or your first childhood crush, there are moments in life, even if they happen when you are very young, that are never forgotten. The first day of JG's was like that for me. I didn't sleep the night before because I was so anxious, but ate breakfast and readied myself for the unknown. Lathered up from head to toe with sunscreen (this was during the days of zinc oxide), we headed to Ponto Beach in Carlsbad. Upon arriving, I saw other kids waiting, looking just as unsure as I was. Mike Bray, Dennis Garrahy, Mike Sylvestri, and John Burns were the instructors—in my opinion, these men were the founding fathers of Carlsbad JG's. They introduced themselves and broke us into two groups based on age and ability. The "A" group was for the older kids who had experience, and the "B" group, where I was, consisted of the younger and less experienced. I suddenly realized that not only was I the youngest JG, but also the smallest by a long-shot. Needless to say, I felt intimidated.

The day consisted of lectures introducing ocean knowledge and hazards, e.g. rip currents, holes, etc.; a morning "vitamin" which consisted of running, swimming, or a combination; swim relays, water raft relays (these were also the days before body boards and paddle boards), lunch, and "free swim". This was, I would later find out, a typical day for JG's. I finished last in all the workouts, lost my raft in the relay and had to do it over, inhaled water when I got tumbled by a wave, and got sunburned on my shoulders and nose. Regardless, I loved every minute and couldn't get enough. The four weeks of JG's flew by, and I was sad when it ended. I was already counting the days until the next summer's session.

When I think back on those first days in JG's, I can't help but think of how beneficial the workouts, competition, water knowledge, and lifesaving skills were to my future. These lifelong skills shaped my persona and gave me a permanent appreciation for the ocean and a job that I still enjoy doing today. As the years of JG's went by, I became more competitive in workouts and got to the level where I wasn't just doing well, but winning! I also felt proud of my younger brothers, who were also enjoying JG's and thriving in their own rights from the training.

After completing six summers of JG's, I was ready for the next step. If I wanted to be a lifeguard, I would first have to become a lifeguard assistant. This was the normal progression from JG to lifeguard back then, and still today. During the time when I was a JG, assistants were paid and had the opportunity to work towers with experienced lifeguards. The tryout for the assistant position was intense and competitive, with 30 people trying out for only ten spots. Also, the tryouts were in April, when the water temperature at the Southern California beaches is usually in the high 50's or low 60's. At this point in my life, I was probably 105 pounds soaking wet. I remember putting Vaseline on my skin and hoping that I didn't get hypothermia.

I remember I came in second among all the candidates, and

my dad told me I'd done a good job and that I'd get that other guy next time! I then had to give an interview—my first ever—and I was extremely nervous answering questions in my only suit and tie. I found out a week later that I was to be congratulated for being offered a job. My hourly wage was $4.50. To me, that sounded like I'd hit the jackpot.

I was 14 years old when I became a lifeguard assistant, and was required to work as near as Carlsbad Beach or as far away as Blacks Beach, 30 miles south. My responsibilities were, in a few words, to do anything the lifeguard wanted me to do from 12:00 p.m. to 4:00 p.m. I quickly realized that lifeguarding wasn't as glamorous as I thought it would be, but I was getting a first-class lesson on going from being idle for a long period of time to suddenly having to push my physical limits to perform rescues. The biggest lesson from the experience was how to be independent and self-reliant. For the entire summer, I had to ride my bike to a bus stop, put my bike on the bus, take it back off again, and ride to my tower. I tried hitchhiking a few times, but my parents found out and after not being able to sit down for a few hours (my dad had a big paddle), I never tried that again! The most valuable part of being a lifeguard assistant was the practical experience. I made some rescues and gained a better understanding of how the public views the ocean. To this day, I still remember my first-ever rescue. It was a 250-pound woman in the waters off Cardiff Beach. It took me a long time to bring her back to shore.

At 16 years old, I was ready to become a lifeguard, and I'd made up my mind that I wanted to work as a beach lifeguard for the State of California. I had done JG's and JG assistant through the State, so naturally I wanted to continue this process. Two things were not in my favor, however, when I tried out in Carlsbad for this lifeguarding position: I had been participating in wrestling during high school and wasn't swimming as much; and cutting weight for wrestling made me even skinnier than I'd been previously (this didn't help in the 57° ocean tryout). I was barely able to finish the swim, let alone do well. I didn't make the cut and was devastated! All those years of building up to that point and then failing… My parents were very consoling, though, and told me I should try out for the City of Oceanside and Camp Pendleton lifeguards. It was a good idea, but I'd had my heart set on working for the State, so these two alternatives didn't excite me.

When the City of Oceanside tryouts came along, I was a lot more prepared physically, swimming every day and not cutting weight. I killed the tryouts. I was first place in the run-swim-run and second in the distant swim. I came out of the interviews second on the list. Again, however, the bubble burst when I was told I was not old enough: I was 16 and Oceanside only hired at 17. Now I was 0 and 2 for lifeguard tryouts, feeling sad and frustrated. Nonetheless, I was ready to try out for Camp Pendleton when the Supervisor of Oceanside Beaches came up to me in the middle of a swim meet. He asked me if I was still interested in working for Oceanside, and I said I was. He quickly let me know that the city had changed their hiring policy to allow for 16-year-olds, and told me to go to city hall and sign the contract as soon as possible. This is how I became an Oceanside lifeguard. I guess everything happens for a reason, because I've been guarding for Oceanside for more than 30 years now.

When I look back at my 30 plus years, I reflect on the hundreds of people with whom I've worked. I'm amazed at how successful most of these lifeguards have become, entering careers as doctors, lawyers, police, firefighters, teachers, etc. The relationships formed during lifeguarding are lasting ones because of the trust you place in each other during rescues and administering first aid. I'm still in contact with lifeguards I worked with 30 years ago.

I like the quote used by Shakespeare in *Henry V*: "We few, we happy few, we band of brothers, For he who sheds his blood with me shall be my brother." To me, this sums up the unique bond that ties lifeguards together. Even with all the treacherous rescues, first aid scenarios, and heroic stories during my years as a lifeguard, in the end it's the faces of the lifeguards I have worked with that come to my mind first.

My Legacy to Oceanside Lifeguarding

I have been lucky and proud to have worked with three younger brothers who were hired after me. The four of us brought an intensity and competitiveness to Oceanside Lifeguards that is still felt today among younger guards. Never have four brothers worked together on the Oceanside beaches this effectively and with such strong support for each other.

Giving back to the Junior Lifeguard program, where I started on this journey, has always been a priority to me. I was fortunate to become a JG instructor in 1993 and took over as coordinator in 1994. I'm proud to say that the program has developed from 40 JG's to the approximately 600 we have currently. The great number of JG's who have gone on to become lifeguards has been one of the biggest rewards. I believe about 90% of our staff were once part of the JG program. I also get a kick out of beating Carlsbad in city competitions on a yearly basis. It seems that life has gone full circle in that regard.

I am currently working as a lifeguard instructor for Miramar College, teaching promising future lifeguards, some of whom have already been hired, as they go through an intense eight days in a physical and instructional academy. As I work with, and give lectures to new lifeguards, who are soon to be sitting in towers up and down the San Diego coastline, I feel privileged and fulfilled by being able to contribute.

All in all, it's been one hell of a ride. As I move toward the sunset of my lifeguarding career, I look with satisfaction at the years past while I anticipate the years to come, when I see a third generation of Wagner's lifeguarding and carrying on the tradition. As they say, "Danger is no stranger to a lifeguard ranger."

CHAPTER 3

PUT TO THE TEST – SCOTT'S FIRST RESCUE

"Experience is the worst teacher; it gives the test before presenting the lesson." ~ Vernon Law

Scott, the middle child – physically he is the most intense and extreme. From surfing Todos Santos to qualifying and competing twice in the Hawaiian Iron Man. He could also be the most serious or the biggest goofball out of all of the boys.

This is Scott's story:

It was the beginning of July in 1985. I was 16 years old, and a rookie lifeguard with only two months on the job. Preceding that had been a grueling course of training during which CPR, first aid, equipment operation, protocols and procedures had been drilled into me over and over, and then a few more times after that! By this point, I should've been feeling completely prepared and confident…but I didn't. *What was I lacking? What did I need to truly be ready?* As I reflect on this, my older self would've reminded my younger self, "To conquer fear is the best way to build your self-confidence," Surveying the same beach I'd grown up on from the top of a lifeguard tower brought me intense exhilaration, and terror at the same time. I know now that what I needed was to be tested, to experience what I feared the most—a real emergency where someone's life was in my hands.

The day had started out in the usual way since I'd started my new job. I arrived a few minutes before 10:00 a.m. with my rescue tube (my "can"), and opened Tower 7 while doing an initial once-over of the beach. Warm weather, no wind, glassy water, waves chest- to head-high with good shape... There were already dozens of swimmers in the water, and even more local surfers. As a lifeguard, I had been trained to watch all areas and people around me, both in the water and on land. My surroundings were like a giant radar screen, to be continually scanned for trouble spots and the individuals most vulnerable to the shoreline's constantly changing conditions. Experienced surfers were not usually a concern, except when they crossed into the swimming area, where they or their boards could potentially collide with swimmers. They drew a significant amount of my attention. I had grown up surfing, and one of my biggest fears was and still is getting nailed by another person's board, or even my own.

By 11 a.m., the crowd had nearly doubled, and the growing number of small children and tourists showed up as giant dots on my mental radar field. There was a small jetty directly in front of my tower, along with a strong current from the south. Because of the larger-than-normal waves, numerous inshore holes and rip currents had formed. I glanced outside of the surf line and noticed a clean-up set coming in, with many surfers scoring some nice waves. After the set had come through, however, I noticed an abandoned board in the middle of the surf-line. My first concern was that it would hit someone as it washed towards shore, but there was no one in its path. Still, I had a bad feeling about the board. *Why hadn't it washed to shore yet? There were still waves coming in!* I took a closer look through my binoculars and then I saw it— the leash was attached and the board was slightly weighed down in back. My gut twisted as I picked up the phone only long enough to say, "I have a 906, Code 3, 200 yards south of my tower, mid surf-line!"

As I bolted out of the tower with my rescue can and fins in hand, I fixated on the board, and shot down the beach in an adrenaline-powered matter of seconds. Popping my can and high-stepping through the surf clutching my fins, my only thought was getting to that board as soon as possible. Finally, I "dolphined" through the breakers, and swam faster than I ever had (which is quick, since I had grown up as a competitive swimmer). When I reached the victim, another surfer arrived at the same time to offer assistance. I dove down into the dark, and followed the leash until I felt the surfer. Wasting no time, I pulled him up to the surface, where the fellow surfer helped me get this young male on his own board. Fortunately, the victim seemed uninjured and conscious, but unresponsive as we made our way towards shore. He coughed weakly in a struggle to gain any air he could. I heard sirens, and finally saw the lights of the lifeguard Jeep. Senior lifeguards rushed up to help.

The young surfer was quickly immobilized and treated for a possible spinal injury, while his vital signs were read, and he was hooked up to oxygen. Recalling the timeline of events, I gave a verbal breakdown of the incident to my commander, Lieutenant McCauley. A brief time later, the paramedics arrived, and took this near-drowning victim to the hospital. Back at the tower with my superiors, I was further debriefed, and assured that I had done everything properly. They applauded me for spotting a rescue that many a fellow guard might have missed.

Throughout the rest of the day, I kept reflecting on the rescue, my part in it, and of course, the condition of the young surfer. As it turned out, he'd had a seizure, but he was going to be alright! Given those circumstances, there was no way I could have been aware of or prevented the incident beforehand. As thoughts of that morning continued to percolate through my head over the next few days, an inner peace, and confidence took hold. For the first time, at least regarding lifeguarding, I knew I had no reason to doubt myself any longer. I had faced my demon, conquered my fear, and I was going to be better for it.

* * *

More about Scott—Never Off-Duty

Scott had just finished teaching his last physical education (PE) class at the local middle school. It was May 2016, and finals week at all the local schools. He decided to sneak out early, and get a surf in before everyone else and their brother got off work, and decided to do the same! It was the first south swell of the season, and he couldn't wait to submerge in the chilly Pacific water after being in the sun all day. Throwing his board into the back of his old sun-beaten Toyota truck, he headed west toward the ocean. The stress of instructing kids all day and fielding their constant questions had taken its toll on him, and Scott was looking forward to his outlet, surfing, and the meditative effect it had on his soul. Driving toward the ocean, he had no idea that instead of leisure and tranquility, this surfing trip would turn dark.

The waves were four- to six-foot, with nice shape. Because it was late spring, the ocean bottom was still torn up from the winter storms. The result was a lot of rip currents. After about a half-hour, though, Scott found his groove and was enjoying himself. The crowd was light and the rides were long. As he sat in the lineup waiting for his next wave, he noticed two school buses rolling into the middle of the parking lot. After his long day with school kids, he thought idly, *Great day for a field trip to the beach, but I'm glad I don't have to watch them!* The students debarked the buses, and moved onto the sand like lines of ants, wearing swimsuits. Some of them carried boogie boards.

Immediately, Scott sensed the riskiness of allowing these kids – who looked to be about nine or ten years old – into the water with conditions like this. There were no lifeguard towers open, and to Scott's surprise, no teachers or parents with a swimsuit on. Scott felt anger building as he watched the group. *These kids were the same age as his daughters! Do those teachers have a clue?!*

Most of the kids playfully started splashing each other, and jumping over small waves in the shallows. Some began to brave the deeper water, trying to outdo each other. Thinking they were fine if they stayed waist-deep, a few of the kids tried swimming, even if only for a few seconds at a time, using a combination of doggie-paddle and something imitating freestyle, but without broad enough strokes to be efficient.

As the swell filled in the coastline, the sets became bigger. Scott noticed after the last wave of a set, that a few of the kids were over their heads. At the same time, he saw surfers heading for the outside to catch the taller waves coming in. He joined them, not wanting to miss out. Scott paddled into the second wave of the next set—six feet and peaky. Taking one more stroke, he pressed both hands against the nose of his board, and jumped to his feet. Scott glided to the bottom, and leaned hard into the wave as he made his turn in the trough. Immediately, he sailed towards the lip of the wave, and cut back sloping the breaking face. The crest of the wave curled out, making itself hollow. Scott pumped his board, and tucked his body, trying to make it through this barrel. Then the entire wave broke in on him, and blew him off his board, into the churning whitewash. Proud of himself for going for it, even though he'd taken a beating, he surfaced, and got back on his board.

That's when he heard the screams. They were coming from outside the surf-line. After ducking the last wave of the set, he popped up and saw with horror approximately 30 kids in the rip current, yelling for help. They were so young! Scott sprang into action, paddling with every ounce of energy he had to the largest cluster of about six children. He yelled to other surfers for help, and most responded. As the scene played out, several surfers appeared with two or three kids clinging onto their boards for dear life.

Scott organized the surfers to paddle into the rip current outside of the breaking waves, and left his board, and the group out there with one of them, the guy who seemed like the most capable, and responsible. He then sprinted towards the kids still in trouble, grabbing, and holding onto them.

By this time, teachers had begun wading out into the water, and screaming. Scott glanced south down the beach and noticed a plethora of red lights, but at this point, only half the kids had been secured. Then he heard a distant humming, and knew things were about to get better fast. Treading water with three children in tow, he saw the black hull and yellow letters of L-41 coming up on him quickly. Scott recognized the WaveRunner operator Matt Mattison. Matt, who had always reminded him of Daryl from *The Walking Dead* with his scruffy face and long hair poking out from under the yellow helmet, was a more-than-welcome sight. "Matti! Over here!" Scott called out. The driver expertly guided the big yellow sled to within inches of Scott's chest.

"Make sure you guys hold onto these handles as tight as you can," Matt instructed the kids. Then he put the ski in gear, spewing water back at Scott as he headed toward shore. He took them directly to the shallow water, where the panicky teachers were gathered.

Lifeguards from the arriving trucks took paddle-boards out with them to maximize the number of victims they could rescue, while Matt shuttled students onto the beach in groups of two or three. The lifeguard boat came on-scene, and Scott instructed all surfers with cargo to get their little victims up the swim step and into the boat. Eventually, 12 kids stood onboard the rescue vessel. The activity continued until every single child had been accounted for.

As a seasoned teacher and coach, Scott was generous with his praise for the surfers and lifeguards who had participated in averting a major drowning disaster. It made him feel good about his fellow watermen, and their capability in carrying out such a well-orchestrated rescue, without losing a single life! Once again, it was a demonstration of the quality of his city's lifeguarding agency, now and always providing a high level of ability on a very limited budget.

But as he headed back towards the beach, Scott made a decision. *He was going to let those teachers have it! Forget being tactful,* he fumed. These were peoples' children, people who believed them to be in good hands! Before they departed, he ripped into them like they were disobedient children themselves. It turned out they were from a private school from Escondido, obviously clueless about the ocean and completely lacking in water safety skills. With their tails between their legs, the instructors herded the traumatized students back onto the buses. Scott looked after them. *Well, at least they all get to go home to their parents.* As always, he felt the reward of having helped prevent a tragedy…or possibly several tragedies.

On a final note, off-duty lifeguards make the beaches and water safer. It has been proposed to the city of Oceanside to give parking passes to their lifeguards for just this reason. Unfortunately, the idea has fallen on deaf ears.

CHAPTER 4

NEAL'S BUSIEST DAY

"You learn you can do your best even when you're tired, and maybe hurting a little bit. It feels good to show some courage."
~ Joe Namath

Neal – my twin brother. Born on the cusp of Aries/Taurus – Neal is definitely the Taurus, and I am the Aries! He is the most laid back of all of the boys, and has the most intuition. He is sensitive, but make no doubt about it he possesses a lot of strength.

This is Neal's story:

It was a hot and humid August day in 1991 in Oceanside, California, during my fourth year as a lifeguard for the city. At this point in my career, I was feeling capable and seasoned, having accomplished many diverse rescues over the past few years. Today there was no breeze to speak of, and the water temperature was in the low 70's. The five to six foot south/southwest swells, however, were creating very hazardous rip currents for the less experienced waders and swimmers. This is something we were all trained to easily recognize. With each set of waves rolling in, the flash rips would appear, and start pulling unsuspecting bathers out to sea, a nightmare for all involved.

I'd had the last few days off, so when I arrived at lifeguard headquarters I was advised about the copious rescues occurring at every location along the coastline within our patrol. Most of the rescues, from what I was told, were happening at the Harbor beach, and on the south side of the Oceanside Pier where main headquarters was located.

Lifeguard Lieutenant Scott Prather told me I would be with him in the lifeguard truck, patrolling the beaches on the south side of the pier. "I hope you're ready to have a landmark day," he said, only half joking. The beaches were certain to be packed, and the surf was building ominously. "We've had mass rescues the last few days…the rips are pulling harder than usual," he went on.

I looked at him, grabbed my can (lifeguard buoy) and fins, and said, "It's hot, the water is warm, and the surf looks fun. Seems like a great day to me!" Thinking back, I believe my experience was working against me, making me a bit cocky as evidenced by my carefree attitude toward a day I would later call "the perfect storm."

At 9:00 a.m., I put all my gear into the truck, and looked toward the beach on the north side of the pier. I noted that the annual national lifeguarding competition was taking place on our sands that day. There were participants from lifeguard agencies all over the country competing in various land and water races. One event that I always enjoyed viewing was the dory boat races. Especially in good-sized surf. It is a sight to behold as the boats try to punch through the surf during the race. The congestion caused by that many boats sharing the same space can make the action literally go "sideways."

If memory serves, it was the boys on the San Clemente dory who unintentionally crashed into the State lifeguard dory on the way back in. Both boats had caught the same incoming wave, but were jostled, and lost control. The San Clemente boat plowed into the State lifeguard vessel which, in turn, hit the pier with a resounding thud. Many of our guards immediately swam out to the collision site. They ascertained that the crew was unhurt, but the boat had sustained a few ripped-off oar locks, and a sizable ding at the point of impact with the pier. It could have been much worse for all involved, and we were relieved it hadn't. Prather walked back to the truck with a grin on his face, and we both silently acknowledged that we had just "gotten off easy" as we set out to make our rounds of all the towers.

Upon arrival at Tower 1, I recognized the two guards on duty, Thorsten Hegberg and Josh Garrison. Both were incredible swimmers, and very gifted athletes; a definite stroke of luck given all that transpired this day. They were wet from escorting several victims out of the flash rips occurring up and down the strand, and bringing them safely back to shore. The tower was a mess...wet sand everywhere, wet towels, wet clothes, food, binoculars, and other debris were scattered about. Thorsten noted my once-over and said, "Yeah...there are two other guards here as well. We've been doing water rotations all day."

They were employing a tag team method of having two lifeguards pull victims from the flash rips, with two other guards on duty at the tower. Each team rested up while the other team actively retrieved new victims, which explained the unusual messiness of the tower. As Thorsten was updating me, I watched the two guards out in the water continuously pulling people from rip currents, and depositing them to points where they could touch bottom, and walk out. As I was evaluating the situation, I witnessed two guards from Tower 3, the tower just south of Tower 1, sprint towards the water to retrieve five more people out of the rip current.

"They've been busy too," Josh commented.

Prather interjected, "Just wait until the tides change, the swell picks up, and the crowds arrive." We all settled into the probability that this was just the beginning of a physically exhausting day.

As we grabbed our cans and fins to assist the two lifeguards already in the water, I realized that we needed to get more guards on the scene. We also needed to start making repeated public announcements from Pier Tower. We did this by utilizing our intercom and speaker system. I was set to assist, and wrangle up more swimmers and body boarders, all of whom were potential drowning victims. As I headed for the shoreline, I could hear my brother Mike in the Pier Tower making those much-needed PA's. Mike was warning bathers not go out past their waists if they were inexperienced swimmers, and to only enter the water south of Tower 3 because the south swell was starting to peak, creating an unforgiving south-to-north lateral current. I knew our rescues would become increasingly more difficult because the rips were getting stronger, and forcing victims farther to the outside, while the northbound current was simultaneously forcing them into the pier. The potential for disaster was becoming more real as the day progressed.

After an hour of reigning in swimmers, body boarders, novice surfers, and whomever else was in the rips, I jogged back to Tower 1 to find four fresh guards waiting there. They had been called in on their off day in response to the sheer volume of rescues necessitated on the south side of the pier. I immediately sent them to the water, as it was an all-hands-on-deck type of day. Everyone was working, and rank wasn't considered as orders and directives were yelled among the guards. Even though our warnings continued over the loudspeakers, I spotted a five-year-old girl in a floatie being pulled precariously into the pier pilings. I was off once more.

As 3:00 p.m. approached, the crowds in the water and on the sand were only increasing. A set of sizable waves was coming ashore as I witnessed yet another large group of swimmers being swept out to sea. The PA's directed at the beachgoers seemed to be having little effect. The Tower 3 guards were all down in the water, continuously performing rescues. Frighteningly, the nature of the rescues was becoming more and more desperate. Swimmers in the rips were now getting "worked" by the waves as they drifted out and towards the pier. Prather quickly got on the phone, and demanded more guards be sent to the area because the number of victims in the water was no longer countable. All guards on the scene were already in the water trying to prevent a mass drowning. Prather quickly swam out to join us in helping to rescue the victims who were in the worst shape. I looked around, and realized that every guard in the water had at least five victims floating with their can.

As we drifted towards the pier pilings, I cautioned my rescuees to remain calm as I safely navigated them through a less-than-ideal path to shore. As we managed to get through the pier unharmed, I saw two lifeguards jumping off the pier to get to another mass group of swimmers in a rip exactly in the location where I had just retrieved my swimmers! I quickly swam my victims in on the north side of the pier, where it was safer to return to shore. Fortunately, all my victims were in good enough shape to exit the water on their own.

I was running back to the base of the pier, and noticed three other lifeguard trucks with Code 3 emergency lights and sirens. All the lifeguards from the trucks were already in the water conducting rescues. When I reentered the water, all I saw were lifeguards, and a mass of victims being canned, or swimmers that still needed to be canned. I began swimming out just as another set of big waves came through, and quickly spotted a body floating face down about 20 yards south of my location. I swam as hard as I could toward the victim, hoping to reach him before the next set of waves came through. This scenario would carry the body out of my sight, and farther out of my reach. When I got to him, I immediately turned him over, and canned him. He was not breathing, and I looked at the Pier Tower, pumped my fist in the water, hoping there was a lifeguard who would see me, and have medics at the beach ready to meet us.

I somehow managed to get him to the beach without dragging him through the pier, or getting clobbered by another set of waves. When I reached the beach, his body seemed to weigh a ton. He was a black man of about six feet tall, with a build of solid muscle. He probably weighed a good 260 pounds. A random thought flashed across my mind that he looked like "Mr. T" - minus the jewelry, and signature Mohawk. In knee-deep water, I was met by a Long Beach lifeguard who helped me lift him to the higher sand, and start resuscitative measures. As soon as we laid him flat, I pressed his neck, found a strong carotid pulse, but he was not breathing. We cleared his airway, and began ventilating him. He regained consciousness after the first ventilation, and began vomiting. The medics from Oceanside Fire got there shortly after. They took him to the hospital for further treatment and evaluation.

As the Long Beach lifeguard and I looked back at the water, we saw there were about 30 guards in the water rescuing more embattled swimmers. All the lifeguards from the competition deduced the growing catastrophe by grabbing their cans and fins to aid us in our efforts to prevent a mass drowning. "This place is frickin' busy, dude!" the Long Beach guard said.

The situation became Code 4 (No further assistance needed) because of the large number of lifeguards in the water securing all swimmers who were in trouble. At last!

As soon as I thanked the guard from Long Beach, I heard a voice come over the PA from the Pier Tower: "If you want to swim, wade, boogie-board, surf, or even get your big toe wet, you need to do it about a quarter mile south of here. If you cannot swim, you might want to call it a day and go home!" I laughed to myself thinking… *that kind of stern but sarcastic public announcement could only be from my brother Mike.* A few moments later, I was surprised to see my brothers Scott and Dave pull up in an LA County lifeguard truck! This day couldn't get any more bizarre. "Dude! LA has a bunch of trucks on our beach. We commandeered this vehicle!" Scott said, with a smirk. "Baywatch is here!"

At the end of the day, I had escorted close to a hundred people out of the water, and that was just me! My "personal best" rescue of the day was my "Mr. T." Medics told me later that he'd been held overnight, but had no lasting effects from his near-death experience.

That was the busiest day of lifeguarding I had ever had, and even today, all these years later, this is still true. It was gratifying that guards from different agencies jumped right into the mix, and instinctively began making rescues on a beach that wasn't theirs to patrol. A few weeks later, our agency received a letter from the Los Angeles County Lifeguard Chief, who happened to be at the competition that day. In his letter, he stated, "The Oceanside Lifeguards did a phenomenal job managing the unmanageable, protecting the lives of countless people." That meant a lot to all of us who were there that day... truly a day for the record books.

CHAPTER 5

TWO BROTHERS AND A BOAT

"Courage is not simply one of the virtues but the form of every virtue at the testing point, which means the point of highest reality." C.S. Lewis

June 1988 - The scariest rescue in my career:

The horizon looked like corduroy; the massive swells were lined up, and coming in as if they were being mass produced at some factory in the middle of the ocean. Closer to shore the breaking waves created the water to move around so violently it looked like the ocean couldn't hold itself in.

It was a southern hemispherical swell from Tahiti that was hitting the coast of Oceanside head on. Oceanside gets consistent surf throughout the year, but since our coastline is facing south, at such an angle that the biggest waves we see are from storms off of places like New Zealand, Tahiti, and Tasmania. These are referred to as ground swells because they are from storms thousands of miles away, and are not generated by local winds. The waves are more powerful, and further apart than a local wind swell. Also, the waves come in sets usually characterized by five or more, and have longer lulls between them than locally generated swells.

The faces of some of these bigger set waves were in the 18-20 foot range. Unlike a lot of big wave surfing spots that can hold a massive swell like this; Oceanside cannot. There are no points or reefs that create channels and give the waves its shape for surfing. So it is usually just big and closed out beach break.

I was assigned tower 16. It is the northern most tower in the Oceanside Harbor Beach, located just south of the north jetty. On the other side of the jetty is the harbor entrance. The waves were breaking all the way across this channel. Usually the water depth is about 25 to 30 feet deep, and waves will only break in water that is comparable to its height. So, a 5 foot wave will not break until it is in five feet of water or less.

My older brother Mike was working a tower down from me in what we call a district tower. A district tower is always staffed with an experienced lifeguard who has at least three years under their belt. They are responsible for a section of beach, and supervise the younger lifeguards next to them.

Besides the massive surf coming in, the day started off pretty uneventful. "June Gloom" was in full control of our weather pattern which is a coastal eddy that basically covers the coast with a heavy marine layer. Only a few surfers managed the courage to surf these big powerful closed out waves. The average beach goers were too intimidated to go past their waste in these conditions.

To pass the time, I picked up the tower phone, and had pier tower (our dispatch) connect me with Mike's tower. Since it was a slow day the dispatcher, and a couple of other tower guards joined our conversation. As the group chat continued I noticed in my peripheral vision a small vessel attempting to exit the harbor entrance. "What are these guys doing" I said to the others. The large surf made this 18 foot boat look like a jet ski.

The boat attempted to get to open ocean as a very large set rolled in. Panicky, the skipper made a frightful mistake and rounded the jetty, and headed towards the beach. Soon, the two men on board were about to feel the almighty power and horror that the Pacific could dish out in heaps. The first wave gently lifted the vessel up, and then passively set it down as if it were a caring mother trying to rock her infant to sleep. The second wave was not as forgiving. Again the boat was picked up gently but once it got to the cresting lip it was violently pitched backwards over the falls of this breaking behemoth. "Send everything I'm going," I mumbled into the phone. *Do I really need to go?* I asked myself. I'm seventeen years old making $13.00 an hour. Why should I? In 1988, there were no WaveRunners with rescue sleds, no scene

34

safety; you were on your own. You were expected to be a man, a waterman who is responsible for saving the lives of those in your water. So yea, I have to go.

My plan of attack was to use the path of least resistance. I decided to run to the end of the north jetty, put my fins on, and time the waves. For the most part my plan worked. After the last wave of a big set broke, I dove in, and started to swim. I swam about 75 yards. I was just about to the outside of the breakers when another set came in. Two very large waves broke just in front of me. My heart was racing, and I started to hyper-ventilate. The explosion engulfed me like an avalanche! I felt like a rag doll being shaken around violently. My limbs were being tossed and twisted in every direction. My body was shoved down so deeply and suddenly that both my ears popped, and my orientation was distorted! *Holy shit! I might die!* I thought. The water was heavy, and so turned up that I could barley propel myself to the surface. My chest felt like it was going to explode as I was now starved for oxygen. I was almost in convulsions as I scratched my way to the surface. Now at the surface, I wanted as much oxygen as possible. Breathing in and out frantically because another wave was breaking right on top of me. The next wave pounded me again. I felt like giving up! This time though, I didn't fight it. I let my body go along with the beating it was being given, and tried to focus on counting. This put me in check. *You've got this Wagner! Go back to your training. Do what you know. Conserve your oxygen, and don't panic. Relax... just swim deep like a dolphin.* I thought. After two deep dives, and some power kicking I was on the outside of the last few waves. I was shocked when I noticed that the strap of my can that was across my chest had been ripped off. Now, I was in the position where I couldn't even rescue myself.

After making it out I had to get my coordinates, and locate my victims. They were approximately 30 yards away. One was hanging on to a surfers' board, and the other was struggling to join his friend. Mike and another lifeguard Luke just swam past the surf, and were on scene.

Mike canned the forty something year old man that was holding on to the surfer. Luke canned the other victim. We decided that we were not going to swim these guys to shore. Instead, swim them out safely another 50 yards so we could put them on the Harbor Patrol Boat. One of the officers on board noticed that I lost my can, and threw me another one.

Luke quickly got his victim to the boat, but Mike was struggling. As I looked on with horror they were drifting dangerously close to the jetty. As I swam to Mike, I quickly realized why his progress wasn't going well. The victim was over 300 pounds, was intoxicated, and had only one lung due to cancer as we would later learn. It was shocking to see a grown man cry and yell "Let me die! Let me die!" It was just as shocking to hear my brother scream out of fear "Shut the fuck up, and kick as hard as you can!" I clipped my can to Mike's, and we started to double swim him out of there. Our main concern was getting slammed into the jetty. As we looked towards the horizon, we noticed there were no waves coming. We put our heads down, cranked our arms, and kicked like hell! Luckily for us, the boat operator took a chance, and picked us up within the surf line. This is risky because he was putting the boat and himself between the large waves and the jetty. If things had gone wrong, the boat could have been slammed up onto the rocks, and busted into pieces just like their bodies would have been. As we approached the dive step at the back of the boat, we handed the victim to the officer's on board, and they heaved him over the rail. Everyone was going 100 mph because of being in the *impact zone*. Mike and I leaped out of the water just as if we were seals hopping onto a dock knowing time is of the essence.

As we entered the harbor on the rescue boat to our surprise hundreds of spectators were lined up on the jetty applauding us. At 17 years old this pumped me up. I felt larger than life! After nearly drowning; I now felt invincible! After this experience of being tested I was ready to concur the world. I felt I proved myself, and could now rub shoulders with the best of the watermen.

After the dust settled Mike called my tower, and complimented me on the rescue. I told him the same, and how scared I was with the risk of sounding like a weak lifeguard who had no business in this line of work. I concluded, "It is too dangerous! I am not doing that bullshit ever again." Both of us laughed cynically because we damn well knew we would do it again if somebody else was counting on us.

Today, as a husband and father, I would have thought a lot more about jumping into these conditions, and putting my life at risk. However, when you are a lifeguard you "just go"! Unlike other public safety jobs that proceed with a plan of attack; we don't have the luxury of waiting, planning, accessing or counting on backup. We just go! These two grown men put themselves into this position. Is saving them worth my family not having me?

Six hours later the high tide receded, and we finally found the boat. It was sitting on top of the Del Mar Jetty. This jetty is located about a quarter of a mile north, and 200 yards further out than where the boat went down. It is also over 20 feet high. This illustrates how much water movement, and massive swell action there was on this day.

***

We have to go but there is no guarantee that we will be coming back...

CHAPTER 6

INSIDE THE LIFEGUARD SERVICE

Quote- "If money is your hope for independence you will never have it. The only real security that a man will have in this world is a reserve of knowledge, experience, and ability." Henry Ford

The Ocean, Currents, and Tides:

It is a tremendous responsibility for a 16 year old kid to be lifeguarding on one of the busiest beaches in Southern California. Thousands of people are on your designated stretch of beach and water. Vigilance and prevention are the most important factors for lifeguarding. It is a very mentally and physically draining job, contrary to popular opinion it's not all about sun tanning and bikini watching.

So, how do lifeguards keep track of everybody? It's actually pretty simple; know where your bad water is, and who your potential victims are going to be. We are the lions, and this is our Serengeti.

Since rip currents are responsible for the majority of our rescues, I feel it is important to discuss them in detail. A rip current looks like a stream or river depending on how big and strong it is. It is characterized by choppy, churning water with a noticeable difference in color, usually more brownish than the water around it. Also, it affects the waves breaking in it. It will hold them up, and delay when they break. Surfers do not like rip currents for this reason.

Usually, the bigger the surf the larger the rip current. They occur mainly as the result of waves breaking on sand bars, creating a higher water level than the area around it. The uneven level of water causes pressure which will be purged into the deeper channel, thus a rip current is developed. The worst time of year for rip currents is after all the winter storms that have taken sand off the beaches, or have added sand near river mouths causing an uneven bottom. Rip currents are very prevalent next to jetties and piers. Most flow 1-2 feet per second, some up to 8 feet, which is faster than Michael Phelps can sprint. Most people drown when they become exhausted by trying to swim directly through it. The best thing to do is relax, let the rip take you out past the surf, and then swim parallel to shore. Once you get down current of the rip then attempt to swim in.

Lifeguards use black and checkered flags, and signs to designate certain areas where people can surf and swim. Surfers are always given the area next to jetties and piers because in general the waves are better there, and they use the rip currents to paddle out in. Rip currents can be good, especially when you want to conserve paddling strength by getting a free ride to the outside. The area designated for swimmers will have a black ball flag; this is a solid black circle on top of yellow background, which means no surfing. The term "black balled" means not allowed. If a swimming area has rip currents, or in-shore holes we will put red warning flags to indicate that on the beach.

Lifeguards are constantly moving the masses to their designated areas. This could be difficult and exhausting with big crowds, and strong currents. Lifeguards need to prioritize. If they leave their tower to move someone in the wrong area, it could be leaving someone else at risk that is swimming where they should be. The neighboring towers help keep an eye on the water whenever a tower guard is down.

Unlike firefighters and police officers, lifeguards spend the bulk of their day preventing emergencies. This is very exhausting work, especially in the hot sun, and dealing with the public. We are educators and ambassadors of the beaches and city. No public safety personnel engage the public and tourists to the extent as we do.

Although rip currents by far are responsible for the most rescues we make, in- shore holes in my experience, are responsible for the most drownings. For small children and non-swimmers these can be silent killers. The ocean is not a swimming pool or lake; the bottoms can be very uneven. People could be standing in waist deep water one minute and be over their head the next. In-shore holes usually can be identified by a break in wave action; in other words a section of a wave will not break in it because the water is deeper than the surrounding area. There is a false sense of security in the ocean; just because you are standing on the bottom you are safe. Some of my sketchiest rescues have been little kids who end up in in-shore holes. They go down quickly. This is why all lifeguards should be able to identify them.

Rescues:

Lifeguarding is a job that depends upon profiling. Contrary to all the political correctness that construes this as a bad thing to do, lifeguards depend on it. When you walk by a tower you are being sized up, and categorized. In general, we hone in on the physically weak, non-ocean people, unattended toddlers, and whoever we deem a risk.

After years of experience I have a few indicators that I use to tell right away if someone is an experienced ocean person or someone that is out of their element. Here are some examples on my list of both:

A more experienced beach swimmer knows how to dolphin under the waves instead of going over the waves. I see the strong swimmer's with their elbows high out of the water. Swimming and playing in the appropriate areas paying attention to the conditions around them i.e. rip currents, staying away from jetties and piers. The lesser experienced person could be wearing t-shirts, cut offs or basketball shorts in the water. It could be something as trivial as having boxers underneath board shorts. Carrying a surfboard a certain way will tell me if you are an inexperienced surfer. Being pasty white, and out of shape, or an unattended child in the water will raise my attention on that individual. Young males have the highest incident of drowning by far out of any other demographic, they tend to underestimate the water conditions, take more risks, and overestimate their abilities.

Sometimes it is not so obvious that someone is in distress or even drowning. Drowning often occurs around a lot of people who are clueless about what is going on. Here are some common signs of someone that needs help; they will always be facing shore trying to get in, or looking for help. Waving their arms, attempting to swim, but unable to get arms out of water, "climbing the latter" - when a swimmer is straight up and down fighting to keep their head above water, hair in their face, screaming, or swimming, but not making any progress.

Oceanside Lifeguards use the Pete Peterson style rescue tube that we call our "can", which is a misnomer. Cans are actually the hard plastic unbendable floating buoy made famous by the early 1990s' television show Baywatch. It is called the Burnside

Buoy. The Pete Peterson style tube is flexible, and can be wrapped around the victim's chest, and then clicked together securing the person. Although most agencies such as Los Angeles and San Diego use the Burnside Buoy, I definitely prefer the Pete Peterson Tube. The last thing a lifeguard wants when making a rescue is a panicky swimmer jumping on them. Potentially drowning them or making the rescue harder than it should be. If a wave is about to hit the victim, the lifeguard will turn the victim towards the breaker, and do a cross chest hold on the victim from their back to make sure they don't slip out of the can. I don't want to have to hold on to my victim, and I want to touch them as less as possible. If the victim is unconscious, or too weak to hold on I can click him into the tube. It is also better for beaches with bigger surf; in general I think it is foolish to use the buoy instead of the tube.

Whenever we make rescues we always let dispatch know, that way other lifeguards will be advised to watch our water, and to monitor the progress of the rescue. We always leave the tower with our lifeguard can and fins in hand. Since rescues usually happen in bad water there is a chance for multiple victims, and additional resources will be called in. Also, the victim might have an emergency medical situation that needs to be addressed. We use hand signals in the water to let guards on shore know what is going on; waving your arm back and forth means that you need assistance, pumping your fist means medical emergency, holding both arms above your head to make an "O" means ok, putting your lifeguard can in the air means you need directions, and making an "X" with your arms means missing swimming or Code X.

Most rescues are made by lifeguards who simply swim out, can their victim, and bring them back to shore. Since there is usually always surf on our beaches, and the potential for multiple rescues we always bring our fins for more power and speed. If victims are out far in rip currents lifeguards use paddle boards which are very effective.

Our agency also has specialized water rescue capabilities such as diving, and swift water emergencies. Oceanside has the San Luis Rey River that can flood during winter rains, and has been a source of many rescues. There are also creeks and lagoons that we have responded to for submerged vehicles and body recoveries. Lifeguards work beyond the beach in conjunction with firefighters on these types of rescues. However, lifeguards will be the ones who enter the water and make the rescue while being assisted from land by fire personnel.

Sea Life:

Human beings are not our only concern in the marine environment in which we work. We constantly deal with sea life being stranded. It is mostly birds and pinnipeds such as harbor seals, sea lions, and elephant seals. In February to March of 2015, we had well over 75 sea lion pups that we rescued on our local beaches and harbor. Our lifeguards got so good at handling these pups that after a while we did not even use nets. We learned exactly how to distract them so we could grab them either behind the neck, or by the back flippers. I will never live down the time years ago when I wrapped a towel around a very small pup that was about ten pounds; I hugged it like a baby and thought it was secure. As soon as I started to walk towards the cage it whipped its head around, and sunk its teeth right into my chest just below the nipple. I freaked out, and dropped the pup right onto the sand; all the tourists were probably very disappointed. At the beginning of each summer when the sergeants and lieutenants are training the fresh batch of rookie lifeguards they use me as their example of how not to handle sea lions.

These freshly weaned pups were malnourished, and for some reason they were not making it on their own. There was not enough bait fish such as anchovies and sardines, or they were too deep for the pups to get. Whatever the reason for this phenomenon Sea World would send a truck up to our headquarters, and transfer them down to their rehabilitation facilities. They would be nursed back to health, and then released into the ocean. By the way, pinnipeds are extremely fowl smelling animals, and the worst of the lot are elephant seals. One Sea World employee told me "they are the only animal that smells worse alive than dead", and also added, "if you are the slightest bit hung over you will probably vomit if you're working around them."

Are there any sharks out there? Of course, it's the ocean that's where they live! According to most shark researchers, late spring on the coast of Southern California is the birthing place for Great White Sharks. This coincides with the beginning of Grunion season. These young pups will stay in these nursery waters, and feed on Grunion, or other fish and rays. Most of the time, when we see Great Whites in our local inner waters they are usually babies and juveniles. There has never been a shark attack in Oceanside, but we have closed the beach a couple times after spotting 6-10 foot sharks in the surf. In 2015, we had a pod of Orca's hunting dolphins right off our coast. It was very alarming to see dolphins literally beaching themselves in terror. That's the thing about the ocean; you never know what is sharing the water with you!

What are our biggest issues with sea life? Most often it is stingrays and jellyfish. To avoid stingrays, we always tell people to shuffle their feet to scare them away before you step on them. If you are stung the best treatment is soaking your foot in the hottest water you can handle. The heat breaks down the enzymes in the toxin, and also eases the pain. The best treatment for Jellyfish is simply flushing the affected area with cool water. Do not rub it, doing so might aggravate the area, and spread the toxin.

Who Knew?

Bee stings actually cause the most life threatening situations at the beach than any other creature. They are drawn to the high tide line by the salt water. Most people are unaware that there are so many bees on the sand while walking bare foot. The problem occurs when one's body over reacts to the stinger or allergen which can cause anaphylactic shock. The tissue in different parts of the body release histamine, and other substances that cause the person's airway to tighten, the blood pressure to drop, and the respirations to increase. Basically, the body's ability to supply oxygen and nutrients to the vital organs (perfusion) is not adequate.

Several years ago I responded to a call for a man stung by a bee. As I drove the lifeguard truck "code three" to Buccaneer Beach, I assumed the patient would have difficulty breathing, and low blood pressure. When I got on scene I thought this person was going to die. His skin was purple, and he was profusely sweating. He was gasping for air, making high pitched wheezing sounds every time he attempted to inhale. His eyes looked big, and seemed to be bulging out of their sockets as they were under some sort of pressure. Drool was dripping down his face onto his chest. *This guy is in trouble,* I thought! His wife was panicking because she had helped him administer his epinephrine that he carried with him for such an emergency. Ironically, she was a nurse, and could tell it wasn't working the way it should. My partner and I immediately put him on high flow oxygen, and elevated his legs.

When paramedics arrived they quickly gave him intravenous fluids, and medicines that support the actions of the heart, and circulatory system. It took several very intense minutes for everything to stabilize this patient! Then, the medics administered antihistamines, and steroids to further reduce systems. I couldn't believe this man might die from a bee sting! These situations are always as intense for the lifeguard as they are for the patient. We never know what the outcome might be.

Anaphylaxis can kill within five minutes. The first symptom is usually the tightening of the throat that is when the 911 call needs to be made. This is truly a 911 emergency. Do not take this lightly after someone is stung, or eats a certain food they may be allergic to.

Next time you are at the beach don't worry about sharks just watch where you step!

*** *** *** *** *** ***

"A team that sweats together sticks together." Unknown

There is an old Kenyan Proverb, "Sticks in a bundle are unbreakable." The bundles of sticks that make up the Oceanside Lifeguard staff are solid oak. The worst summers we have are the ones that are not busy because of bad weather, small surf, and few medical emergencies. When the south swells pump in, and we are up to our elbows in water rescues our staff builds up a cohesive bond that is hard to break. In general, we love when all hell breaks loose, that is when you rely on each as a team, and you prove yourself as an individual.

Just like the city itself the Oceanside Lifeguard staff has an edge to them. The beach is "our house" and we have more pride in our agency than any others I've been around. Our tryouts are tough, and our staff holds each other to the highest standards. Introverts not willing to give their all will be weeded out quickly. This is the Wild West! Marines, gangs, drugs, and addicts all find their way to the beach. That's why we have a reputation for being "cowboys" that have each other's back. We are not co-workers but brothers and sisters! The average lifeguard excelled in sports like water polo and swimming, and were serious students.

Here in Oceanside, we are not the overly funded, huge budgets of bigger agencies like Los Angeles County or San Diego City that have all the bells and whistles. Our resources are limited, so that means our level of responsibility, and risks are higher. Oceanside lifeguards have to evolve into a jack of all trades; part lifeguard, cop, EMT, mechanic, and construction worker. We are always on stage, and in view of the public eye. We are not behind closed doors sitting in a Lazy Boy chair playing video games and watching TV.

Since our agency does not have a lot of room for vertical advancement, our full time staff is relatively small. The cast of characters working down on the beach is made up of mostly college students and a hodgepodge of other professionals such as firefighters, teachers, police officers, engineers, and even some doctors and lawyers. There have been several lifeguards that have moved on to Special Forces in our military such as Navy Seals, Air force Para Rescue, Coast Guard Rescue Swimmers, and Marine Recon. It's a hot bed for recruitment because of the mental and physical toughness of our lifeguards. We work in an uncontrolled environment with every situation being different, and variant ways to go about getting the job done.

When a rookie lifeguard first walks into our headquarters the red carpet isn't rolled out for them. They are expected to tread lightly, and earn their rightful place in the pack by proving themselves. Lifeguarding requires extreme physical fitness, vigilance, and the understanding of your surroundings. You are judged by the entire staff by your lifeguarding abilities first and foremost, it trumps every other personal quality you have. If you are a crappy lifeguard but are good at operating the WaveRunner; you are just a crappy lifeguard on the WaveRunner.

After a while we all learn each other's strengths and weaknesses. Once we expose someone's soft underbelly we constantly go after them like a pack of hyenas. The more upset you get the worst the treatment gets; the best advice is to laugh along with the others. You must have thick skin.

Every morning most of our staff will work out or PT together. Most of the work outs are a combination of running, swimming, or paddling, and when the waves are big bodysurfing. If you do not participate, or are way behind the pack you will be looked upon as weak.

Every year we send down our best athletes to Coronado to compete against the rest of the county in a lifeguard relay competition called the Pirate Olympics. We would always dominate, even against the City of San Diego, which has roughly four times the amount of guards we have in Oceanside. Our grit and determination usually makes the difference. The thought of losing is hateful to Oceanside lifeguards.

Women make up roughly ten percent of our staff. They are held to the same standards as the men, and they are also judged for their lifeguarding abilities. There is almost a sorority feel to them inside the bigger fraternity that encompasses the rest of the staff. The men are protective brothers to the female lifeguards as we are one big family.

One summer, the female staff was very divided over swim suits. Some of the ladies were wearing skimpy red Brazilian cut bottoms. This caused public complaints, and some of the other women thought it made them all look bad. A special committee was formed between the two camps, and they had to agree on a few styles of suits that they all felt were appropriate. Most of the staff was entertained by this drama. However, it was a real issue, and for some the final resolution was a compromise of a more conservative suit. Together the bond of their sisterhood elevated them above this, and lifelong friendships were made.

Some of the funniest pranks I have ever witnessed have happened down at lifeguard headquarters. There has been the typical putting jellyfish in people's lockers, sand crabs in each other's sandwiches, to just all around horse play. But the funniest one I can remember was between two lifelong friends who grew up literally across the street from each other. They new each other well. For the sake of this story we will just call them Tom and Andy.

One nice summer afternoon, Tom was running relief; he was in charge of giving each tower guard a 30 minute break. When he got to Tower 3 he noticed that his good old pal Andy was there. Tom informed Andy that he could begin his break. After Andy left, Tom noticed a note indicating, if you want to play the am/fm radio you have to find the hidden battery. It was agonizing trying to find the battery, and manage the water at the same time, but after 20 minutes he found it deep in a storage compartment above the door.

Once Tom started to relax to some music he began to think of a plan to get back at Andy. So, for the next ten minutes he went to work. Andy came running back after spending 30 minutes at headquarters. "Dude, you're right, there are some hot girls here today! I like the brunette in the white thong!" Andy said excitedly. "So, I see you found the battery," he added with an amused grin. Tom just laughed and headed towards pier tower to give them a break up there. After a few minutes in the air conditioning Tom saw that Tower 3 was calling up on the switch board. "Hey, how long did it take you to find the battery?" "Not that long, oh by the way, Andy does your face tickle right now?" Tom asked. "Yea it kind of does, why?" "Look at the phone." Ugh! The sound of laughter made the fishermen look up at pier tower with curiosity. It seems that before leaving the tower Tom unscrewed the mouth piece of the phone, and threaded dozens of pubic hair through the small holes.

The saying is true, "Idleness is the workshop of the devil." Another time at headquarters, we had a bunch of wiffle ball bats that were supposed to be dropped off at Jr. Lifeguard headquarters. One evening before a hand full of us were about to leave, we turned off the lights in the locker room shower, and the unsuspecting guards in there soaking themselves after a long day were given a code red. (Attitude adjustment) We went to work with the bats, they didn't know what hit them. They sounded like a bunch of school girls screaming as they tried to guard against the onslaught of hits. The next day we were all laughing as the victims proudly showed their bruises. Please don't confuse this with bullying or hazing, in our world this is considered bonding! They would eventually pay us back throughout the summer.

The most memorable pranks I have seen throughout the years on the lifeguard staff most of them happening in the early 1990's (today's generation might not be able to handle them) here are a few of my favorites:

- Cups of urine being put on locker room doors that would pour down on unexpected lifeguards entering.
- Laying down on the sand in front of your friends tower, and urinating through your trunks onto the sand. Then crafting it into a "piss ball", and throwing into your friends face!
- The grossest one I have seen was a lifeguard who shit in a bag, placed it into a friend's locker who had been off for 3 days. Upon returning, he found it had dripped, and oozed all over his uniforms, and belongings...
- The victim of the prank above, without care, stuck his finger up his ass, after taking a crap... walked up to his friend, and wiped his nasty finger across his upper lip giving him what is referred to as a "Dirty Sanchez"!

Every summer there is a lifeguard house that everybody hangs out at. This is where the younger guards start building lifelong relations with some of the best friends they will ever have. Some will drink their very first beer, while others will spark a summer romance that they will forever remember. They all have something in common; they are fit, educated, good looking young people with the best summer job in the world. They have no mortgages or kids; these are the years that some day they will all yearn for. Sometimes, I reminisce on my first few summers of lifeguarding, and realize that I was truly blessed to of had those experiences.

Rookie parties were once a rich tradition that gave the first year guards an opportunity to give the senior guards a collective thank you for helping them survive their first summer. Each rookie would pitch in a couple of hundred dollars on food and beverages. They would serve the other guards in appreciation. Years before cell phones, we would make fliers, and hand them out to the most beautiful girls on the beach.

Today, this tradition has been lost for several reasons. It reflects the times, and where our society has gone. Parents of some young lifeguards called and complained that their kid was "bullied" into throwing a party, or some of the rookies feel they don't owe anybody anything. I think to summarize it best, back in the day it was like the movie Dazed and Confused. It was all an accepted ritual of making that leap into adulthood.

Lifeguarding with my brothers Mike, Scott, and Neal made it that much more special. We pushed each other, and brought intensity to the staff. When other lifeguards would first meet us they couldn't believe how competitive we were, and that we would fight each other at the drop of a dime over a game of basketball or football. All four of us had each other's backs, and we still do to this day!

It is a great feeling that I can go down to lifeguard headquarters on any given day, and find someone to workout with or to go surfing. At the beginning of each summer it is exciting to see everyone again, and to learn what they have been doing throughout the year.

Before I conclude this chapter there is one very important item I left out; Burritos! We go through thousands of burritos at our meeting room table every year. Burritos are to lifeguards as donuts are to cops! Breakfast burritos, California, mixed, surf and turf, fish, the list goes on; this is the fuel of the gods. We know which place makes the best, which gives you the most quantity, and who has the best salsa! Some of our most important issues have been discussed in depth with a burrito in one hand, and salsa in the other.

CHAPTER 7

THE WORST WAY TO BE INJURED IN THE OCEAN

"How to make God laugh. Tell him your future plans." ~ Woody Allen

During my first few years of lifeguarding, I attended a program called Project Wipe-Out at Hoag Hospital in Newport Beach, California. This is a spinal injury prevention program designed to educate first responders, and the community about potential dangers at our beaches.

Newport was the perfect place for a program like that, because when I think of Newport Beach, I think of The Wedge. The Wedge is a bone-crushing wave that jacks up out of deep water, and breaks in the shallows. Newport Beach is a world-famous body surfing spot, but notorious for creating this kind of wave because of its topography.

Newport, Huntington Beach, and Oceanside are all very busy places to lifeguard in the summer primarily because all of them face south. When storms develop in the South Pacific, they produce long-interval ground swells that hit these beaches. Newport is unique, however, in that the continental shelf drops out quickly compared to Oceanside. At the end of the Oceanside Pier, the water is about 40 feet deep; at the end of the Newport Pier, which is only half the length of Oceanside Pier, the water is 90 feet deep. In general, waves do not break until they reach shallow enough water, so for example, the water must be no more than 4 feet deep for a 4-foot wave to break. The waves in Newport come out of deep water, and suddenly hit shallow water, which "jacks up" the waves, throwing them violently onto the sand. This is why Newport has what is known as heavy shore break, and consequently, a higher frequency of spinal injuries among swimmers and surfers.

Beaches in general have a high incidence of accidents resulting in spinal injuries. People run into the surf and dive headfirst into the sand. Some go over the falls of a breaking wave, and get pile driven into the bottom, and others dive off their surfboard into sandbars. Unwitnessed near-drownings found close to shore are assumed to be spinal injuries, and as a rule treated with the appropriate precautions.

At Project Wipe-Out, lifeguards from all over Southern California crowd into a conference room to hear the latest on head, neck, and back injuries. Speakers included medical specialists in neurological and spinal trauma.

"The spinal cord is the consistency of a barely cooked spaghetti noodle," one speaker explained. "It is protected by about 20 vertebrae. If one of those are fractured, it could easily cut the cord, which is why it is important to immobilize the patient as well as possible." He then revealed some of the eye-opening statistics regarding numbers of people becoming paraplegic and quadriplegic from some type of surfing accident. The large numbers blew me away!

Throughout my years lifeguarding, I've responded to dozens of victims with actual, or potential head, neck, and back injuries. Some of them died instantly. Some sustained permanent injuries, and others were probably fine, but since we don't carry an x-ray machine we have to assume they are injured. We "package up", or immobilize, any swimmer who hits their head on the bottom. Using a technique called PMS (pulse, movement, sensation), we take the pedal pulse in each of the victim's feet to see if they are equal, assess their movement by asking them to wiggle their toes and squeeze our fingers with their hands. We check for sensation by squeezing one of their toes, and have them identify which one without looking. It is important to palpate the back of their neck and back for deformity, ask if they have any pain, check their pupils to see if they are dilated equally and reactive to light. If they have blacked out or lost consciousness, we automatically "c-spine" them, meaning we immobilize their neck in a rigid cervical collar.

I have pulled people out of the ocean who were not fully oriented, and bleeding from the top of their head. We are trained to put a backboard behind them and lower them onto the ground. Frequently, people with head trauma are violent, or demonstrate repetitive questioning, e.g. "What happened?" and then a couple minutes later, "What happened?"

I recall a chilling incident on an October day one year. The ocean temperature was still relatively warm, not much surf, and the water was flushing out to sea preparing for a negative tide at 2:30 p.m. Earlier that day, I'd gone on a 3-mile paddle, then treated myself to a carne asada and egg burrito. Later, I took the lifeguard truck out for a long patrol of the beach, feeling content.

At the same time on a different section of the beach, two friends were paddling out during the halftime of a Chargers football game, frustrated at the score, and wanting to burn off their negative energy. This would be their last time surfing together.

The call came in over the radio, "NorthComm-2184. Drowning at 900 The Strand, south."

"Wow! I wonder if this is a legit call." I exclaimed to my partner as we activated the emergency lights and siren, and raced to the location. As we approached the scene, we saw a lifeless-looking body being dragged out of waist-deep water by another surfer, and a lifeguard. We drove the truck right up to the victim, and my partner jumped out, and grabbed the oxygen. I got the backboard and Stokes basket (a compactable rescue assembly used for immobilizing, and transporting trauma victims) from the truck racks.

We lowered the unconscious surfer onto the backboard, and tried to determine whether he was breathing. Water was pouring out of his nose and mouth, his skin was slightly purpled and blotchy. We found he wasn't breathing. My partner checked his carotid artery for a few seconds, he felt a weak pulse. Using spinal precautions, we carefully opened up his airway by thrusting his jaw forward without moving his head. As I sealed the mask over his nose and mouth, my partner compressed the air bag to send fresh oxygen into his lungs. The victim had a scalp wound about the size of a silver dollar on the front top of his head. Right away I knew that one of his cervical spinal nerves had been compromised.

After immobilizing him, we carefully carried him up to The Strand, where we met the paramedics. My partner climbed into the ambulance with one of the medics, and continued airway management. After another medic started an IV, the fire captain decided to land Mercy Air at the turnaround in the Harbor beach. Near the parking lot there is a large, slightly elevated circle for landing helicopters.

Several lifeguard trucks were used to cordon off the whole area to make way for the rescue helicopter. Once the air ambulance landed, a trauma nurse got out, and immediately began to assess the patient.

When the surfer regained conscious, he began to panic in disbelief. It was hard for me to watch him crying…he hadn't deserved this. A physically fit, good-looking guy in his early 30's.

He could've been any one of my brothers, friends, or me. The nurse wound up putting him in a chemically induced coma to help stabilize him. The world as he knew it was over. The friend he had been surfing with, who had helped pull him out of the water, now had the responsibility of making probably the worst phone call of his life: to notify the victim's family what had taken place.

Witnesses said they had seen him dive off his board, and then float up. I have become over-the-top adamant about telling anyone who will listen—NEVER... EVER... dive off your surfboard! I constantly lecture everyone I care about how real this is. If you get sucked over the falls of a wave, just tuck into a ball, and cover your head with your arms. If you must dive, land on your belly, sticking out your legs and arms like a starfish.

Sadly, the last I heard about this surfer was that his neck had indeed been fractured at C3, resulting in his being a quadriplegic. He was in a special treatment center, reportedly suffering from severe depression.

This incident really put things in perspective for me, giving me an even deeper understanding of the expression, "Don't sweat the small stuff." Most of the time, we take our health for granted. It may seem like a drag having to fix things around the house, take out the trash, or even get out of bed early to go to work, but thank God you can do these things! Seeing how quickly a life can change is a strong reminder to get up off the couch, or away from the desk, do something physical...thrive and live! Never take a day for granted. It could be your last!

CHAPTER 8

THE SUMMER OF YOUNG LOVE

"One day your life will flash before your eyes, make sure it's worth watching."

It was the summer of 1991. I was only 21 years old, and full of myself. I was young, fit, olive skinned, with a swimmers build. My body had finally filled out from the skinny guy I was in high school. I had a full head of brown hair that I let grow out while away at college. It was a bit shaggy, but I thought it looked cool. My testosterone was raging through my body and I felt on top of the world! Lifeguarding was on my mind, but so were girls!

I had just arrived home from college, and just like my older brothers did, I would stay with my parents and was eager to start lifeguarding. The thought of warm sand between my toes and the sun beaming down on my shoulders was a welcoming thought after the long, wet winter I had experienced up at Chico State.

The beach cruiser in our garage hadn't been used in quite a while. I inflated the tires, dusted off the cob webs, and rode it down to lifeguard headquarters. This half mile jaunt took me through my old stomping grounds. *Wow, had it changed; or is it just me?* I see the faces of my neighbors growing older, fresh graffiti on some buildings, and more unkempt yards than I remembered. Maxson Street used to be thriving. Kids playing ball, skateboarding, and the dads all took pride in grooming their yards. Now, it seemed unfamiliar. As I got closer to the beach, the old familiar smell of salt air greeted me. I parked my cruiser, and the sound of the cracking waves was my welcome home. This was the time to work as many 10 hour shifts as possible. I will be stock piling money for my senior year. This would be the *"fat"* I would need to survive on during those brutal winter months. There is only so much mac 'n cheese, top ramen, and frozen damn burritos w/sour cream and melted cheese I can frickin' eat! This is my senior year after all, and let's face it I will be spending a ton of money in the bars.

To let everybody know I was back in town. I rode my bike in the garage of lifeguard headquarters, down the hall, through the meeting room, and straight into my Sergeants office without stopping. My front tire was an inch away from his desk, as he looked up at me like *what the hell dude!* I smirked, and simply said "Hi!" – Like Stewie, from Family Guy! "Wags, you better get your tire away from my desk, or I will get my knife and slash it.", he said. "Take your pansy ass bike, and head up to Tower 12. That's where you're at today!" I thought to myself, *Damn, I'm in a tower!*

As I backed out I envied the older guards. They had earned their EMT certificates, and had the luxury of driving around all day in the yellow jeeps. They looked "set" cruising down the beaches with their Ray-Ban shades on, and arms stretched out over the steering wheel all chill. I imagined them cruising by beautiful girls sun bathing out in their G-strings. I was green with envy.

Tower 12, was located in the Oceanside Harbor. A more family oriented beach for the most part. Sometimes we'd get lucky and spot a beautiful gal all by herself. These distractions took some time to get use to as a young guard, but never, ever, got boring!

It was approaching 2pm that day, and I saw a lifeguard jeep pulling up to my tower. They were coming to relieve me of my duties. We were allowed one half hour. This was the time to take a power nap on the warm beach right in front of the tower; especially if a guard had too much to drink the night before. Other times, it was a time to take a nice swim in the ocean to stretch out our legs from being cooped up in the tower all day.

"Hey Neal!" I said, to my twin brother as he got out of the jeep to relieve me. Tower guards were sometimes aloud to ride as a passenger with seasoned guards. It wasn't often available, so, it was Neal's lucky day. Neal took over watching the tower for me while I took a quick swim. After bodysurfing a few waves I was feeling refreshed and rejuvenated. Then, it happened! I spotted a bombshell. I couldn't help but notice this hottie in her black bikini with a mesmerizing rock necklace. She was thin but voluptuous. She had long, thick, dark brown hair that ended just above her waist. It had a beach wave that naturally formed from getting it wet in the salt water. It looked sun kissed and glistened in the light. Her olive skin was beautifully tanned. When she looked up at me as I was coming up from the surf, I couldn't help but notice her unusually large cat eyes. Those gorgeous eyes reminded me of a Disney princess. Lashes so long they looked like fluttering butterfly wings every time she blinked. *Damn! She is gorgeous and naturally exotic looking*! I thought to myself.

As I climbed the ladder on the lifeguard tower, I said to my brother, "Dude, do you see that girl over there? She is gorgeous!" Neal replies, "Dude, you don't recognize her? That's Jennifer, the "Gothic Girl" that went to "the other school" in town, as he rolled his eyes. Don't you remember her showing up with her friends when people from the two high schools would have house parties?" "Damn dude! That's her? I was so rude to her at those parties. God! Look at her now... She is so beautiful!" "Good luck brother, she might be hard to catch," Neal said. "However, I may be able to stoke you out. I heard she runs around with Motor's girlfriend Donna. So, you may want to hit him up!

Motor, was my off road buddy. He literally took after the character in the Muppet's Show "Animal." Neal and I would call on him when we were looking for a bit of excitement in our lives. You could be sure of it, if you called Motor you would be signing up for a good time! Sometimes more than you bargained for! Hence, he has the name Motor, always running 100 MPH. He had this old 1969 Ford Bronco that he would take off-road from time to time. One of the favorite spots in the area to go was at Calaveras Lake. The days before the area evolved into a landscape of Southern California track homes. If there was no surf this is what the guys would do in the 90's. Kick up some dirt, and take an off-road ride through the untouched back country. One time, when Motor was driving us all in his Bronco, I remember him taking things to exceptionally extreme levels. I thought to myself, *Hell, he just may roll this thing*! Sure as shit, that is exactly what he did! Luckily, all of us jumped out right before the Bronco rolled down a hill, and got stuck in a ravine. When he got home, he started calling everyone he knew that could possibly tow his ass out. Off-roading after all, was illegal, and Motor didn't want his parents or the authorities to find out he rolled the Bronco. If my memory serves me, the Bronco stayed down in that ravine for months before he finally figured out how to tow it out.

I decided to give Motor a call to see what he was up to, and let him know I was back for the summer. After shooting-the-shit I asked him if he wanted to hang out. He told me, "Dude, I'm hanging out with my chick tonight. We are having a campfire and barbecue at the Carlsbad State beach camp grounds." He added Neal and I should head down with our girlfriends. Neal had a girlfriend. He was dating a girl from Humboldt State. Her name was Karen, and lived in Huntington Beach with her parents during the summer. She would make the trek down in her VW Rabbit with a license plate that read, "KARROT". It should have read, "PARTY GIRL" because she was always the life of the party! She loved hanging out with Neal, and his lifeguard friends. She always made sure everyone had a good time. I told Motor I didn't have a girlfriend but asked him if he knew of a girl named Jennifer? "You mean Jen? Motor said. "Of course, I know her! We went to high school together and she is best friends with Donna. Matter of fact, Jen, has been invited to the campsite tonight. You should show up tonight and hang out Brother!"

I couldn't believe my luck! You better damn well believe I will be there! I quickly called Neal, and told him to head to the campgrounds. I then packed up what I could find in my parents garage that I might need for a campfire. Within an hour, I was headed for Carlsbad.

When I showed up, Motor was there with Donna, and Neal was there with Karen. Jennifer was nowhere in sight. I was bummed! I didn't know if I should ask Donna if she was going to show up. I didn't want to reveal too much that I was hot on the trail for her girlfriend. The guys poked fun at me for not having a woman at my side, but I took it like a man. I cracked a beer, and settled in around the campfire for the night.

It was the days of no cell phones. So, it was basically a waiting game to see if Jennifer would show up. I decide to walk to the bathroom to relieve myself from all the beer I was putting down my throat in anticipation. Walking back from the bathroom I look around, and still no Jennifer. It was going on 7:30pm. I probably should just pack up, and let these two sets of love birds have their evening together. Just as I was giving up all hope that Jennifer would show, out of the darkness I heard this sweet voice. "Donna, I'm so sorry it took me so long. I had a hard time getting away from work tonight." And there she was, stunning as ever, even after a long day of work, hugging on her best friend. All I could think was, *I sure hope I get one of those tonight, and maybe with a little luck, more!*

I thought, *Game on! It's time to make my move without coming off like I want her too much. But, damn this was going to be hard!* She was keeping her cool too. Donna filled her in that I liked her. Jennifer had remembered how rude I was to her in high school. So, it was," game on" for her as well. She was ready to make the evening especially difficult for me if I came off in the slightest bit like a jerk.

The guys were starting to cook up burgers on the barbecue. I thought this would be a perfect time to show her I was a true gentleman. I noticed that the picnic bench was wet from the evening dew. She was about to sit down and I told her to hold on. I gathered some newspapers left over from making the campfire, and laid them down for her to sit. Hoping this gesture would score me some points. Smiling and flirting with those big cat eyes, she says, "Well, aren't you quite the gentleman?" *Alright Wag's, don't screw this up with your mouth. Just smile and stay cool.* And that is exactly what I did.

After we ate, I asked her if she would like to take a walk with me down to the beach. It was a magnificent evening. Clear as clear could be, a warm breeze, and the moon was extremely large that evening. She said yes. We proceeded toward the staircase that would take us down to the beach. We sat for a long while in the middle of the staircase just talking. We both had those butterflies we all experience when you know you are feeling something for the other person you are attracted to. Our hands just gravitated towards each other without us even thinking about it. However, we were both still trying to play it cool. It was a strange moment. We slowly made our way down to the beach, where we stood on the sand hand in hand facing each other. *Dude, here is your moment! Do it, give her that first kiss!* But I couldn't. My courage deflated, and before I knew it she was leading me back up the staircase. *Dammit, you idiot! You just lost your chance! I am going to do it; there is no way she is going to leave tonight without a kiss from me!* It was now around midnight, we were making our way up the stairs. I could see the full moon light beaming down on us. *Wow, this is perfect! I have another shot.* As I lean in for the kiss, and about to touch her lips... out of nowhere in the darkness of the night, came this guy hauling ass on a 10 speed bike! He lost control on the loose gravel, fell to the ground, and made a huge dust bomb all over us. The guy proceeds to profusely apologize to us both as he gets up off the ground. Just then I realize *wait a minute, why does that voice sound so familiar?* I looked at him and yell, "Running Idiot... Is that you?" He looks at me and said, "Surfer Dave? What are you doing out here?" He looks over at Jennifer, then, he quickly realizes what I was up to, and high tales it out of there as quickly as he arrived.

Running Idiot was a college buddy of mine. He got the nickname because he would get high, and take extremely long runs for hours around the college campus. No one could ever understand how he could smoke so much dope, and get straight A's, albeit, his major was Botany.

For whatever apparent reason, it seemed fitting for our evening to end without a kiss but a good laugh. My time for that kiss would come a few nights later, down below the Carlsbad cliffs, on a blanket, around a bonfire on the beach. Our moment was perfect, just me and her under the light of the magnificent full moon.

I know fate was forever responsible for that first evening. From that evening on, we spent the next five years learning to be each other's best friend. The memories, the stories, and the friendship we made along the way; all, forever to be etched in our memory. In the summer of 1995, I got down on one knee around a bonfire, near Tower 12, in the Oceanside Harbor, and proposed to that beautiful girl. The same place I first laid eyes on her so many years before.

CHAPTER 9

THE FOURTH OF JULY 2007 – LIFEGUARDING ON WATER AND LAND

"The mob has many heads but no brains." ~ Thomas Fuller

Lifeguarding can be a very frustrating job, especially if you embrace the theory of Social Darwinism for the betterment of society. Don't get me wrong—I'm not a callous or insensitive guy. But, there are a lot of weak and unintelligent people whose genes would have died off 150 years ago if it weren't for the compassionate nature of modern American society. Instead, these people are thriving today with a higher-than-average birthrate.

Beach communities are havens for the homeless, druggies, alcoholics, eccentrics, gangsters, and just about every type of person you can imagine. The masses move in crowds like flocks of sheep without bothering to read signs, watch their children, or be aware of their environment.

These are the type of people who trip over curbs while texting, or hit the car in front of them because they are adjusting their radio. They are also the type of people who fall asleep on the beach while their three-year-old is playing in the water. It amazes me how people walk right past a "Danger – Rip Current" sign, and swim right in front of it despite the big red flags attached to it. Doesn't it ever seem odd to them that they are the only person swimming among a pack of 40 surfers? Psychologists would have a field day researching human behavior from a lifeguard tower on a busy beach.

One day, I was sitting in Pier Tower with another lifeguard, monitoring the crowd on the beach. I was astounded by the number of people swimming right next to the pier in a surfing area despite the signs, and numerous public announcements (PA's) broadcast from the lifeguard station. "Look at all the Muppets down there," my fellow lifeguard commented. "Yeah, and that makes us Statler and Waldorf," I responded. For those of you who've watched the Muppets, those are the grumpy old hecklers in the balcony.

Lifeguarding on the 4th of July is like playing second base in the World Series. The crowds are massive, the energy is pulsating, and lifeguards are in the middle of the action. Families arrive as early as 3:00 a.m. Some, actually, never leaving from the night before just to reserve their spot on the sand. The areas around the city-designated fire pits, with a view of the fireworks are the most coveted pieces of real estate on the 4th of July beach.

Drinking begins early, lasts all day, and continues into the night. The walkway on the upper part of the beach, called The Strand is packed with bicyclists and pedestrians at various levels of intoxication. The parade of humanity including all the people who've donned outrageous, skimpy outfits becomes a fascinating spectacle for all. But when late afternoon hits, the fun, energetic crowd changes to reflect a darker, more menacing human element.

There were a few 4th of July holidays in Oceanside that attracted the true plebeians of society. The crowds resembled the yard at San Quentin with bikini-clad females mixed in. During those years, most seasoned lifeguards felt it was all a matter of time before "the shit hit the fan." And so it did in 2007…

I recall this particular 4th of July vividly. The piercing buzz sound of my alarm clock jarred me awake early that morning. As I reached to shut it off; the red digital numbers reminded just *how* early: 4:00 a.m. I was on stake duty this morning. This means I had to get down to the beach by 5:00 a.m., and stake off emergency access lanes for our trucks next to each tower in my district. I fumbled around for the t-shirt and shorts I'd put out the night before. I grabbed them without turning on the lights, and dressed in the hallway not wanting to wake up my wife. Rising from downstairs was the welcoming and comforting smell of coffee. I had strategically programmed the coffee pot's auto-start for morning. After pouring this hot liquid fuel into a travel mug; I put on my backpack, slid into my sandals, and grabbed my Mag flashlight. But, as I was headed for the garage; I heard my wife coming down the stairs. "Be careful riding your bike in the dark, and don't get hurt trying to be a hero today, either," she said. "I love you," she whispered as I gave her a hug and a kiss. Then replied, "I love you too. Have fun today, but don't come down to the beach with the kids. It's too crazy."

After a three-mile bike ride; I arrived at our headquarters. No personal vehicles were parked in the lot. This was going to be our command post for the day. Blake and Ryan were already working, getting all the WaveRunners and IRB's (Inflatable Rescue Boats) operational. Blake had a shit-eating grin on his face as I coasted my bike into the garage. "We got a south swell. There's already a large crowd on the beach… I hope you're ready for a busy day!" A large tarp had been set up at the entrance of the garage with tables and chairs underneath it. All our medical supplies were spread out on the tables. This was where we'd be servicing our walk-in medicals, and hosting what was sure to be a great number of lost children throughout the day.

After changing into my uniform, I walked into the staff meeting room, and met up with my assigned partner for the day. "Dave, we are staking out all the emergency accesses in district three this morning," Ian informed me. Ian was an unassuming type of guy, not loud or showy, just a solid lifeguard. A good athlete and all-around waterman. He was one of the better surfers on our staff. Ian's best quality was his IQ, though. I thought of him as the "Dr. Spock" of our agency—very logical and unemotional.

We loaded our personal gear and equipment for our staking duty into one of the lifeguard trucks. Then headed about two miles south of the pier to District 3. After an hour-and-a-half, we brilliantly engineered some of the best emergency accesses our four most southern towers had ever seen.

Driving on the sand, heading back towards headquarters; I heard someone yell out my name when we were drawing near the Oceanside Pier... "Wagner!"

I told Ian, "Hey, go pull up to that guy. Let's see what's going on."

It was my old friend Chris, who I'd known since we were kids going through the Oceanside school system together. "Hey, what's going on, Chris? What are you doing down here so early?" I asked.

"I'm producing a video about Oceanside on the 4th of July," he replied with a grin on his face. Chris was an entrepreneur who'd dabbled in music producing, promoting, and now, it seemed, video production. He was also the first African American friend I'd ever had going all the way back to kindergarten at Mission Elementary School.

"Hey Man," Chris remarked, his voice beginning to sound tense. "These white guys are trying to kill me!"

"Alright, what did you do to piss them off?" I joked.

But Chris wasn't smiling. "No, seriously! These guys legitimately want to kill me. They tried to run me over!" Just as he said that, I looked up to The Strand, and saw what appeared to be a souped-up 1971 Oldsmobile with several guys inside. The car was shiny black, with chrome rims and beefed-up tires. It looked mean. The windows were tinted dark, and smoke was coming out of the front passenger window which was rolled down halfway. Just then, all the doors opened nearly simultaneously, and four guys stepped out. They looked like members of the Aryan Brotherhood, just out of the "pen". Beefy and muscular, most likely from years of prison yard workouts. They all had shaved heads, and were tatted from head to toe. One wore a swastika tattoo which stretched from his armpit to his hip covering most of the left side of his body. These guys were intimidating!

They started walking towards us, yelling every racial slur you could imagine. "Chris," I asked anxiously, "are you sure you didn't piss these guys off? Because they sure look mad!"

"No," he replied. "I just wanted to get them on my documentary, so I started filming them."

I knew Chris was a pretty good ocean swimmer. I'd seen him body surfing up in Humboldt County on a road trip we took to visit Neal in college. "If these guys start getting froggy," I said, "let's head for the water. Who knows what weapons they might have?"

Ian spoke up. "We won't have to do that. The police are pulling up right behind these guys."

Within a minute, there were five patrol cars surrounding the Oldsmobile, and all the cops had their weapons drawn. After detaining all four men for a few minutes, one was arrested for a parole violation and was facing a third strike felony charge. The other three were sent on their way, but managed to give us dirty looks before continuing south down The Strand.

I let out a long breath. "Hey Bro," be careful today." I told Chris.

"You too!" he answered. "This place is no joke... that's why I'm down here documenting things though."

Meanwhile, Ian stood by looking like he was trying to soak everything in. "There is a weird vibe down here today," he remarked in a low voice. "Something bad is going to happen."

The next 11 hours were filled with non-stop water rescues. We had multiple people get slammed into the pier pilings because of the relentless lateral shore current pushing south to north. At the Harbor beach, the rip currents were a quarter-mile long and 50 yards wide. Dozens of victims were retrieved at a time using WaveRunners, the IRB, paddle-boards, and good old-fashioned swimming. Most lifeguards did not have a chance to get dry all day. By the end, 361 rescues had been performed.

Around twilight, our captain wanted to have a briefing with all the unit operators, i.e. personnel driving the trucks. "I want everyone in pants, boots, and long sleeves," he commanded. "Also, make sure all of you have mag flashlights. We need to go pick up all the tower guards, and get them back here safely." Our captain had an uncanny way of knowing when trouble was about to happen. His biggest priority was the safety of his lifeguards.

The aroma of barbecue filled my nostrils as I walked toward the lifeguard truck. Ian stayed back at headquarters to leave more room in the truck for the guards I would be picking up. Before getting in, I glanced south to gauge the crowd, both on the beach and The Strand. It looked like a human cattle drive. Sand, dust, and smoke filled the air as more people herded into this location trying to get a prime viewing area for the fireworks show starting in roughly 40 minutes.

Tyler had a worried expression on his face as he stood by his truck with his partner Forrest. "Damn, dude," Forrest said to me in his usual greeting. "This place is racially segregated like that prison show *Lockup*," he noted with a nervous chuckle. "All the homeboys [Hispanic gang members] are on the north side of the pier, the Samoans are in the beach amphitheater participating in our Sister City Celebration, some African American gang members are hanging out at Tyson Street Park, and the White Supremacists are partying at the southern end of The Strand." He paused, and looked around edgily. "And to top it off, there's one of those cheesy street carnivals right above us on Pacific Street."

Once I got into the truck I realized how hard it would be to drive anywhere with this many people. I had to wait for a break in the crowd to merge onto The Strand from the beach. Before I could make my move; I heard a bloodcurdling scream from the crowd.

A tornado of humanity came straight towards me as I looked south down the street. Dust was levitating around a thrashing whirlwind of arms, fists, legs, and bodies engaged in a massive brawl. The altercation fragmented into four or five smaller fights which rumbled their way north like the human waves fans make during stadium football games. There was no way I could move the truck without hitting someone. The fight was coming right at me! I decided to bail the truck and get back to headquarters asap!

"All lifeguards get into the garage, and take cover under the cement ramp." I heard our captain yelling as I got closer. Our lifeguard headquarters is located underneath the base of the pier. It is bordered by at least a foot of concrete—the safest place available if bullets started flying. We took shelter as the fight surged on, and moved to the north side of the pier.

About five minutes later, the Oceanside Police cleared us from our staging area. Looking around, I saw wounded people lying everywhere, like images from the Civil War once the dust settled.

"We need backboards," a fire captain yelled. Three people were being attended to on the south side of the pier. Ryan grabbed the backboard from my truck as I grabbed the medical supplies, and we headed to the north side parking lot.

I knew the battle would be ending soon once I got sight of about 40 cops in riot gear surrounding the entire area. In the middle of the police circle were four severely wounded people. A friend of mine named Blake, who had been a lifeguard, but then joined the Oceanside firefighters/paramedics was attending to an unconscious African American male in his early 20's. The man had apparently been kicked in the head several times while on the ground.

"Blake, what do you need?" I asked.

"I'm trying to start an IV on this guy, but his friend is making matters difficult." Blake replied. The gangster-looking friend was amped up, swearing, jumping around, and not giving Blake the space he needed. The last thing Blake wanted was to get stuck with a needle because some jackass wouldn't back away.

"Get out of here!" I commanded the other male.

"What you going to do?" he responded belligerently.

Without hesitation, I grabbed him by the collar of his shirt, and shoved him to the ground about five yards away. "If you don't back off, I will have your ass arrested," I said angered.

He hesitated, sore about the fact that he'd just been manhandled, and wanting more than anything to reassert himself. But after looking around at the massive police presence, his better judgment took hold, and he decided to leave, although not before yelling a few choice words at me.

Around that time, I noticed my boots were sticking to the

pavement from all the fresh blood in the parking lot. I took a moment, and looked around trying to fully assess the situation.

Nearby was a young African American female who looked about 17 or 18. She had been stabbed under the armpit. *Hopefully the brachial artery hadn't been punctured.* I thought to myself. Because if it had she could bleed out quickly. The medics continued to treat her while a battalion chief ordered us to get our lifeguard trucks.

No ambulances could get down to our location beneath the pier. We loaded the patients into our trucks. With Ryan accompanying me; we were responsible for transporting another African American male who looked to weigh about 250 pounds, and was in stable condition despite being stabbed 16 times!

I half-joked to Ryan, "Hey, isn't it interesting that none of these gang members died? If it were an innocent, law-abiding citizen, they would've died for sure."

The police had two people in custody. One of the suspects was a teenaged Samoan girl who was bleeding profusely from a stab wound to the knee. The other was a Samoan man roughly 30 years old who had a torn-up shirt, and taser wires attached to him. Sweat dripped down his forehead as he tried to get his breathing under control. The man had a wild look in his eyes; like a warrior just after battle.

A dozen cops marched in front of the three lifeguard trucks that were transporting the wounded up to Pacific Street. A temporary Incident Command was set up to triage the five trauma victims, two of whom were being transported up from the south side of the pier. Ambulances from neighboring cities had arrived to aid the city's expended emergency resources. Three of the intensive care emergency victims were ultimately flown out by air ambulance.

The firework show started, but most of us were not interested—it seemed anti-climactic after what we'd been through. The real show had just ended, and most of the participants were going to the hospital or jail. Before going off duty that night, all us lifeguards involved with the incident were debriefed at headquarters. The police informed us that there had been an ongoing feud between a local Samoan gang, consisting primarily of "Bloods," and an African American gang who were mainly "Crips." The feud had begun over a recent neighborhood murder in the deep valley.

Ever since this incident, lifeguards have joked that our city is on lockdown on the 4th of July. For this holiday, the police chief has established what we refer to as a "no fun zone," an area within two blocks of the beach where no alcohol, bikes, skateboards, fireworks, etc. are allowed. All fines are tripled in this zone, and the area is saturated with police officers. This strategy has actually been effective, and Oceanside's 4th of July has been restored to a family atmosphere. This is the way it should be. Unfortunately, the fireworks show has been cancelled indefinitely.

All of us thought our busy day would've been big local news, but there was not a word of it on television, or in the newspapers. Instead, the headline-grabber of the day was something about drunk college kids starting a fight on a beach in San Diego!

CHAPTER 10

SUMMER THEMES OF LIFE AND DEATH

"The clock of life is wound but once,
And no man has the power,
To tell just when the hands will stop,
At late or early hour...
Now is the only time you own.
Live, love, toil with a will.
Place no faith in time.
For the clock may soon be still." ~ Robert H. Smith

It seems like every summer has its own theme—like individuals with their own unique persona. Some are defined by the sheer number of rescues, others by spinal injuries, boat rescues, or beachgoer violence. The summer of 2006 was infamous for the number of CPR's we had to give on our beach.

It was July 3rd, and the tourists walking along Oceanside's long wooden pier were amused by watching four lifeguards on the beach, pushing a WaveRunner set on a small cart with balloon tires down towards the water. Once it hit waist-deep water, the driver, wearing a large float coat and helmet, revved it to life. The jet wash threw back a violent stream of foamy seawater as the lifeguard throttled the machine, and plowed through the inshore waves. He maneuvered the WaveRunner over and around several waves while heading farther out. Spectators undoubtedly coveted the thrill and adventure of such a ride.

As someone with a lot of hours on WaveRunners, I can say with all honesty that it loses its appeal quickly. It's fun to ride and jump waves...until your lower back starts aching. The constant, wind-driven ocean spray on your face is maddening! Your eyes get fried from the salt and sun. You are soaking wet for hours on end, and after a while start feeling like a soggy piece of beef jerky.

That was my condition while patrolling on the WaveRunner that particular July 3rd. The sun was piercing, the waves were small, and I was bored out of my mind just bobbing around in the Pacific Ocean with nothing to do. This all changed in an instant, however, when a sudden call came over the radio! There had been a drowning at the Cassidy Street beach.

My adrenaline kicked in as I squeezed the throttle. The wind and spray of water lashed my face and torso as I violently bounced over waves. The random thought crossed my mind: Scotty from *Star Trek* saying, "I'm giving her all I got, Captain!" It was a turbulent ride, but I was determined to get there first. As I flew in towards the beach, I saw two men in red trunks dragging a motionless girl out of the water, and onto the sand. My WaveRunner slid to a stop as I ran it up to ankle-deep water. With drownings, it's best to have as many first responders as possible on scene, so I bolted over to assist the other lifeguards.

The victim was a good-looking female in her mid-20's, with sandy-blonde hair, and an athletic figure. She was wearing a wetsuit. As I looked towards the water, I saw her abandoned surfboard washed up at the tide line. What had happened? She'd been found in waist-deep water, but the waves weren't big, and she was most likely a decent swimmer. It didn't make sense.

The lifeguards who had reached her first determined that she had a pulse, but was not breathing. A bag valve mask now covered her mouth and nose as we began giving her positive pressure ventilations. Two more lifeguards appeared, with one carrying a backboard, and the other an AED (Automated External Defibrillator). Because it had been an unwitnessed drowning, we were mandated to treat her as if she'd sustained a spinal injury. We were careful not to move her head, neck, or back. We also log-rolled her onto the backboard so we would have a hard surface to work on.

My brother Neal arrived on the scene with his partner Cory. Cory was the supervisor on scene. He made sure everybody was in position, and doing their job. He is usually very mellow, almost having a nonchalant attitude about things. As he assessed the situation, and looked down at the non responsive girl he took it to heart. She was not going to die on his beach. Cory, a former All American Water Polo player is about six feet six inches tall; he towered over the crowd, and he radiated authority. When he directed people to do things they quickly snapped to attention. Neal is a paramedic, so he took control of the patient's airway. He attempted to put an oropharyngeal airway down her throat, but the high volume of sputum and saltwater coming up made this impossible. An oropharyngeal airway is a plastic tube used to provide free passage of air between the mouth and pharynx of an unconscious person. He then decided to put a nasopharyngeal up her nostril, which basically accomplishes the same thing, but would be out of the way so he could suction her airway to clear it.

As we continued to give her emergency airway management, I noticed that her blue eyes looked glazed-over, and were slowly rolling back into her head. "She doesn't have a pulse!" a lifeguard yelled. *Just like in the movies*, I thought. *Right now, she is clinically dead*. Instinctively, I grabbed the trauma sheers, and cut off the top of her wetsuit. It was time for CPR, and hooking up the AED. I dried her off with a towel, and my partner connected two electrodes, one onto her upper middle chest, and the other at the lower left side of her torso.

AED's are very easy to use, as they are designed for the layman. Each electrode has a diagram of where it is to be placed on the patient. The AED will detect if there is a shockable rhythm such as ventricular tachycardia or ventricular fibrillation. In both these conditions, the heart is electrically active but in a dysfunctional pattern. The AED itself advises step by step what to do next. "Stop CPR, assessing patient… shock advised, stand clear!" The most important thing to remember is to have no contact with the patient when there is a shock being delivered, because it could result in the person administering it to have cardiac arrest. "Everyone clear! I'm clear! Everyone clear!" Cory, said loudly. He delivered a shock. "Continue CPR," the machine advised.

As Neal continued to suction her airway, another guard was preparing to ventilate her. At this point, I continued to bend over her torso with extended arms, administering one-and-a-half to two-inch chest compressions. I was doing what her heart was supposed to be doing—trying to circulate oxygenated blood throughout her body.

After another minute of CPR, the AED advised it was assessing the patient again. "Shock advised, stand clear!" "Is everyone clear? Stay clear!" Cory called out, and then delivered another shock. This was followed by another minute of CPR, and another shock.

When the paramedics arrived, they started an IV with cardio-stimulant drugs, mostly epinephrine. Almost instantaneously, we picked up a slight pulse. As the medics continued their work, we carried her up to the back of the ambulance. An air ambulance landed at a nearby park, and she was flown down to University of California San Diego (UCSD) Medical Center, where she was put on life support.

After two days in the hospital, this girl walked out completely fine. The doctor on duty attributed her full and speedy recovery to the quick response time after she stopped breathing to when she was given oxygen. In addition, the combination of CPR, the AED, and cardiac drugs were imperative to her being brought back. So, what had happened? How did this young, healthy, athletic girl drown? A surfer walked up to me later, and told me he had overheard two young girls on surfboards talking out in the water. Reportedly, one of the girls said she might have hit somebody when she wiped out on a wave. If I had heard this, those girls would have been talking to the police, and been held accountable. The apparent apathy on the part of whoever said that sickened me. How could they not have looked to see if the person they'd hit was alright?

* * *

It was just two days later...July 5th, the day after the holiday.

Typically on this day, the beach is trashed, everyone is hung over, and enthusiasm for working is minimal. My own morale was especially low, because I was again scheduled again to be on the dreaded WaveRunner. It's not that the WaveRunner can't be fun, but if the surf is small, and there isn't much going on, a shift can seem like an eternity.

So, there I was, bobbing around again, mentally preparing myself for a dull day. Then the call came, "L-41 respond to North Coast Village for a possible drowning." *Another one?*

Ten minutes earlier, a tourist from Arizona hopped in the water, excited about her first ocean swim in over a year. Wearing her favorite pink swim cap, she made some final adjustments to her goggles to ensure they had a tight seal. She looked towards the horizon, and softly palpated the slight bulge above her left breast as the waves lapped against her legs.

The cool saltwater invigorated her as she dove through the surf. Being tossed around by the waves made her feel alive again! She felt good, even though months earlier she had been given a new pacemaker to help regulate her heartbeat. The heavy sea air filled her lungs as she tried to get her breathing into a rhythm. She was well past the breakers when she felt her heartbeat skip, slow, and then speed up again. A sudden wave of terror gripped her as she felt the beat become erratic. Turning towards shore, she waved her hand to signal distress. This would be the last thing she remembered.

The guard on duty, Brook, was feeling good that morning as she sat in Tower 8 sipping her morning coffee. *Another beautiful day at the office*, she thought to herself. A great runner and swimmer, Brook had always wanted to lifeguard. She had proven her skill and motivation while she was a Junior Lifeguard, dominating in competitions up to the national level. Now, she scanned the beach and water, satisfied that her signs and flags were all in the right spots, and the coned-off emergency vehicle access next to the tower in place.

She began to contemplate what her morning workout was

going to be. Looking out over the ocean, she concluded she would go on a nice, long swim… like the lady who was already out there. *Is she waving to me?* Brook thought, as she gazed out past the surf. But the waving stopped, and Brook saw the woman hunched over face down, floating just above the surface.

There was no time for communication to Pier Tower. Brook knew that just knocking her phone off the hook would ring Pier Tower, and make them aware of a possible emergency. The neighboring tower would then be called to assess the situation. "Dennis, is Tower 8 okay?" a voice echoed through the phone. Dennis immediately looked over, and noticed that Tower 8's can was down. Scanning the water in front, he saw Brook running out with the strap of her can around her chest.

"Holy shit," Dennis exclaimed. "There is somebody floating out there. Respond a unit. I'm going to assist."

Brook honed in on the pink, partially submerged swim cap as she swam through the surf. Once she got to the victim, Brook wrapped the can around her waist, and clipped it. She propped up the swimmer, who was unconscious and unmoving. There was foam coming out of her nose and mouth. Brook looked towards shore, and saw a parade of yellow trucks with red lights, and began to pump her arm up and down, signaling that this was a medical emergency.

Dennis arrived on the scene, and clicked his can onto Brook's, giving them double the swimming power. The surf was small— about two-foot, "mushy" waves with not much power. This can be both good and bad; good because it's easier to hold onto a victim, especially an unconscious one. On the other hand, the swim in takes longer without the push toward shore.

When they reached the shore, they heard the familiar hum of my WaveRunner, which would've been a lot more useful if I had arrived a couple minutes earlier. Other lifeguards were hustling about getting the oxygen and the AED ready to go, while the swimmer was immediately placed on a backboard. Compressions and oxygen were administered.

I landed the WaveRunner, and ran to assist the other lifeguards. Remembering the situation two days earlier, I grabbed a nasopharyngeal, rotated it up her right nostril slowly, twisting it to ensure the bent part was going towards her mouth. This allowed us to suction her airway with less obstruction. Somebody attached the electrodes of the AED, and after two minutes of CPR a shock was delivered. When medics arrived, the patient had received three shocks, and she responded positively to epinephrine, and other medications.

This whole incident was almost a carbon copy of what had happened two days before! After some time in the hospital, the woman was released with no lasting effects of her drowning. The defective pacemaker, which had either failed or misfired, was replaced.

A month later, the two women came by lifeguard headquarters to meet all the lifeguards who had saved their lives. The news media was there, and it turned out to be a touching moment. Just a couple years before this, we hadn't carried AED's, but what a difference this made! Both these near-drowning victims had been given a second chance at living.

I have to wonder if this experience changed these women's outlook and attitude toward life... Do they still "sweat the small stuff" like most of us do almost daily?

* * *

A Few More Tales and Truisms

These women had been lucky, because much of the time when we do CPR, the outcome is different. It all depends on how quickly life-support treatment is administered to someone who isn't breathing.

Tragedies like the following happen also:

The day before I started lifeguard training as a rookie lifeguard, a 16-year-old boy from Temecula came to the Harbor beach with his friends after getting out of school early for finals.

The waves were a solid six to eight feet high, and he decided to jump off the jetty with his body board right as a big wave broke on him. His friends never saw him surface. My brother Mike was part of the Code X search which failed to find him. It shook Mike to the core when he saw the boy's mother show up to the beach, and melt to the sand with pure heartbreak. The next morning, all of us rookies had to swim in that area to look for the body. Eight days later, Harbor Patrol recovered the boy's bloated body. The only remaining skin was on his nose.

The oddest drowning in my career was when two friends in their 40's decided to go snorkeling off the north jetty in eight-to-ten-foot surf. Really? They had weight belts and wetsuits on, but during a set of waves, one of them panicked, and grabbed onto his friend. Fearing for his own life, the friend let go of him, came out of the water, and called 911. The surf was too big for a line search. So, about ten of us jumped off the jetty, and swam south with masks on. Twenty minutes later, we found him, and brought him in. Sadly, he was pronounced dead by the medics on the beach. The fire captain ordered that he be placed in the back of a lifeguard truck; where he lay for six hours until the coroner arrived. An intimidating sight, to say the least; feet sticking out from under a blanket in the back of a lifeguard truck parked in front of big surf.

Then there are the rescues of Marines. Usually, they are either assigned to Reconnaissance or training for Recon. The ones not familiar with the ocean put themselves in bad situations. It's amazing to me, but some of them can't even swim! I figured all Marines had to know how to swim! One busy afternoon, I recalled seeing a Marine who looked like an NFL linebacker, walking around on the beach. I didn't think anything of it until I later heard there had been a drowning between Towers 2 and 4. They gave a description of the missing swimmer, and it sounded like the same muscular man I had seen. The Marine apparently thought he was safe in waist-deep water, but he didn't know about inshore holes. Within a few steps, he was over his head. Witnesses said he went down like a rock. We did a Code X search for three hours, until the sun went down. His body was found nine days later, two miles south, and one mile out from where he had been last seen.

Late spring /early summer is the most dangerous time of the year for beachgoers. At this time, swimmers are not used to the ocean, out of shape, and the bottom is torn up from winter storms. This creates rips and inshore holes. To top it off, lifeguard staffing is limited until Memorial Day weekend. Years ago, in mid-May, a tourist was visiting from Washington state. Overweight, and with probably had no clue about the ocean, he decided to swim at the Harbor beach, which is known for massive rip currents. On the day the tourist was there, the surf was breaking five to seven feet, and no lifeguard was on duty in the tower. The man became exhausted, not knowing how to get out of the rip current. One of our lieutenants witnessed him struggling, and swam out to him, but when he was still about 20 yards away, the swimmer went down right in front him. The lieutenant dove down, searched, but could not locate him.

My brothers, a couple of lifeguard friends, and I had been surfing, when our captain got on the Pier Tower PA, and told us to come in. "We need lifeguards to do a body search at the Harbor! Get your gear and get up there," he told us. After trying to do an organized Code X line search for about ten minutes in the big surf, we all decided to just bodysurf, and let the current and waves take us. Maybe we would stumble upon the body. This worked! Scott dropped into a good ten-foot face, and as he was getting pummeled by the whitewash, he bumped into the submerged man. Scott waved and yelled to all of us, and we retrieved the body, now lifeless.

There are some bodies we never recover, like the guy who walked to the end of the pier, ordered food and drinks, and instead of paying his tab, left a note saying he was going to kill himself. He proceeded to put a backpack full of weights on himself and jumped off the pier, never to be seen again.

Most of the time when there is a drowning, we find the body right away. One evening, while a group of us were working. The late shift team was washing up the trucks. A lady ran up to us screaming that there were three people drowning on the north side of the pier. Sure enough, one was actively struggling, and two of them were going under. We managed to get all of them in, and had to do emergency airway management on one who was not breathing, but had a pulse. We thought we were all heroes until two days later, when we found out that they had taken him off life support and he had died. This is always disturbing news to receive.

In my experience, when surfers die in the water it is usually the result of a heart attack, or spinal/head trauma. Swimmers usually drown because of exhaustion, or by overestimating their ability in rough conditions.

There are a few variables which allow some drowning victims to float longer than others. Wetsuits and a higher percentage body fat help with buoyancy, in addition to how much air the person has left in their lungs. After a couple of minutes, most bodies will submerge a few feet underwater. If the body is not found right away, it resurfaces after decomposition sets in; which produces gases that make the body extremely buoyant. This usually occurs six to ten days later. If a body is still not recovered by then, it submerges again once all the gas is gone, and the body has filled with water. At that point locating a body is difficult. The current and wind play a large part in where the body drifts.

Recovery is, quite frankly, super gross. Most of the skin of a drowned person has been removed, or is in the process of wearing away to the point you can't even identify what race they were. Usually there is an oily, greasy slick of water around the body. It is so massively bloated that the person's features are extremely distorted. To retrieve the corpse, we carefully position a Stokes basket with buoys attached to it, and try to scoop them into it. We do not get into the water with them if we can help it.

CHAPTER 11

CRASH!

It was April 29, 2007, and the time of year when the air vacillates uncertainly between cool spring breezes, and hints of summer warmth. The chilly ocean water off Southern California acts as a natural air conditioner, creating a hazy marine layer as it greets the hot wind blowing in from the desert. Memorial Day was at least a month off, meaning one thing to all of us offseason lifeguards: the privilege of surfing during break-time to satisfy our mandatory daily workout. No small blessing that day—three- to four-foot, fairly shaped waves with a southwest swell. Not epic waves, mind you, but definitely worth taking a ride on.

I was thinking if I waited one more hour, the water might be less crowded, and the tide more surf-worthy… that, plus hoping the wind wouldn't pick up. Such are the random thoughts almost so automatic that they're unconscious of a surfer on the shoreline hedging his best bets. I stared out at the lineup of surfers, and was anxious to get my turn, but continued my patrol just south of the Harbor beach; waiting patiently until 10 a.m., which I'd decided would be the most optimal time to get my ride.

An hour before this—not too far away—a new mother in Carlsbad was hugging her mother, sister, and stepfather goodbye after a much-appreciated family visit. They had come at such a joyous, yet exhausting time for this first-time mom. Whom, was still getting acclimated to her new role, which was proving to be rewarding and challenging. The luxury of having both her sister and mother around to help had made the transition a little easier. So, saying good-bye was especially emotional for all of them this time.

The stepfather was an experienced pilot, who had recently purchased a new plane with the intention of making their visits from Arizona more convenient and frequent. As her family loaded the last of their luggage into the car, the daughter's eyes moistened, and her nose tingled as she fought back tears. She wrapped each of them in a fierce, and slightly prolonged hug. Thus, showing not only her gratitude for their help, but her great love for them all. After her baby was passed around and "loved on" one last time, all three family members got into the car. As it pulled down the driveway, she gave her final wave with a hint of sadness. Unbeknownst to her, fate would intervene on this day.

The house seemed disturbingly quiet as the new mother began to process the void. Her husband was a Carlsbad State Parks Lifeguard, and had left the house hours earlier for his shift; leaving her alone with the baby for the first time in days. "Well, it's just you and me kid," she said aloud, smiling as she looked down into her baby's eyes.

In yet another scene close by, Pete and Ben were enjoying their usual Saturday morning fishing trip on a boat about a mile off the landmark Encina Power Plant in Carlsbad. Both men were sergeants in the Marine Corps, stationed at nearby Camp Pendleton. Ben was thrilled to have his eight-year-old son Steven onboard, as this was Steven's first time in a boat on the ocean. Although the fishing was slow, Steven was still enthralled tormenting the sardines in the bait tank.

At 9:30 a.m., the Cessna 182 Skylane revved its engines preparing for takeoff. The captain, accompanied onboard by his wife and stepdaughter, accelerated west along the asphalt runway at McClellan-Palomar Airport. Within seconds, the plane rose hundreds of feet into the low clouds hovering overhead. Roughly two minutes later, for unknown reasons the plane started to plummet.

"Reel up, let's check your bait," Ben said to his son Steven.

The boy's eyes grew wide. "Dad, look at those slices on the sardine. I told you I had a bite!"

"That's from a halibut, my friend," Pete remarked. "They sorta slash their prey when they bite. Let's go out to about 80 feet, and drift over the same ground again. Maybe we can get 'em this time!"

Pete put the boat in gear, and the motor hummed as the vessel moved another 500 yards out to sea. Then he cut the engine, and allowed the onshore winds to push them into a drift towards shore.

"I think we'll get one on this pass," Ben said optimistically.

The serenity of the ocean calm offered a needed refuge for these combat-inured war veterans. Its vast quietness a welcome contrast to the violence they'd seen in Iraq and Afghanistan. Here on the water, there was no chaos, just soothing peace, and an opportunity for personal reflection. To Ben, it was also precious bonding time with his son, with whom he'd had little opportunity to spend quality time due to the rigors of active duty.

As they patiently waited for their first catch of the day, Ben went down into the cabin of the 30' Grady White fishing boat to retrieve the sandwiches he'd made for the crew. But before he could open the ice chest, he heard Steven scream "Daddy look!" Ben was startled and unnerved by the pitch of his son's cry.

Hearing the strained roar of the plane desperately trying to recover from a nosedive, Pete and Steven looked up, and followed the vessel in horror as it plummeted into the water about a mile off-shore. It made a thunderous crack as it hit the unyielding surface, like a major-league ballplayer breaking his bat, except infinitely louder, and more ominous. The initial impact created a huge splash, sending out a frothy surge of wake. As the plane broke apart, each piece of debris, including large sections of both wings, skipped across the water like flat stones. The heavier parts sank slowly while the more buoyant pieces came to a rest, and bobbed around with the swell.

Peter lost no time in grabbing the boat radio. "Coast Guard, we have just witnessed a plane crash. We are approximately one mile west of the Encina Power Plant. We have just witnessed a plane crash," he yelled into the microphone.

The most crucial emergency radio frequency which lifeguards routinely monitor is VHF channel 16. This frequency is monitored 24 hours a day by coast guard agencies around the world, as well as all civilian sea-bound vessels.

Moments before the crash, I was still preoccupied watching some of the better surfers in Oceanside near the south jetty, pushing me to drive to headquarters, and paddle out. *After this Steely Dan song is over*, I thought, *then I'll go.* "Babylon Sister" was playing as I sang with the lyrics. *"Well, I should know by now... Like a Sunday in TJ... That it's cheap but it's not free... That I'm not what I used to be... And that love's not a game for three."*

The emergency distress over channel 16 broke through the backup singers' chorus *"Shake it..."* There has been a plane crash off the coast of Carlsbad a mile west of the power plant! *Did I hear that right... a plane crash? Holy shit,* flashed through my brain. *Oh My God, we are the closest agency equipped to handle this emergency. We had to coordinate quickly!*

Kellen was in another lifeguard truck at the Harbor beach, so I decided to contact him, and enact a plan. This was not particularly easy in this type of unprecedented emergency. We decided to rendezvous at the Harbor Patrol dock with a couple HP officers, and to board Rescue 1, a Crystal Liner boat designed for emergency operations. We would be the first responders to the scene while our dive team prepared their gear, and boarded Rescue boats 2 and 3.

Once onboard, the Harbor Patrol officer meticulously plugged the coordinates into the GPS system, and as we headed out of the harbor my mind was racing... *How many people were on board? Were there any survivors?* Still, I was subconsciously preparing for the grim likelihood of what lay ahead. Plane crashes are notoriously not survivable, and that knowledge was curbing my usual optimism.

As we raced towards the scene of the crash, we noticed a fishing boat, and WaveRunner circling around it. The smell of fuel, salt, and blood-iron filled my nostrils as I surveyed the glossy gray surface of the ocean, now gleaming with rainbow spectrums from the large quantity of fuel displaced from the aircraft.

The debris field was disturbingly eerie to take in, like nothing I have ever encountered before. Damn, in my 20 years of lifeguarding, and the extensive training I have received nothing had prepared me for this horrific scene.

When we neared the boat, we observed two U.S. Marines onboard, and two long, blanket-draped forms next to them on the deck. The Marines had already pulled two deceased victims from the wreckage, and were respectfully blanketing their bodies like a medical examiner or coroner would. Brownish-red, blood-saturated water sloshed around everywhere on deck, and it was immediately clear this was no longer a rescue, but a recovery.

The man on the WaveRunner was an Encinitas lifeguard, and with the help of the two Marines, had gotten the two female victims' bodies onboard. Since we didn't know how big the plane was, or how many possible victims there were, we continued to search the debris field for more casualties. Among the floating wreckage were pillows, blankets, bags, tires, and a shoe. There were no other bodies within sight; we surmised that if there had been other casualties, they had submerged with the larger sections of the fragmented aircraft.

Within a half hour, a Coast Guard cutter from San Diego was on the scene. We gratefully turned over incident command to them, as we were out of our depth in effectiveness at this point. The bodies were put into bags, and transferred to the cutter. I could tell from the apparent ages of the victims, and their physical likeness that they had been related. Most likely mother and daughter. This brought thoughts of my own wife and daughter to mind, and I sadly acknowledged that someone out there was going to be devastated by the news of this crash. The Coast Guard contacted McClellan Airport, from whom it was learned that there had been three people onboard the plane at take-off.

Rescue 2 and 3 showed up on scene with six divers. The Coast Guard determined that the crash site was over an underwater canyon, the depth of which was 120 feet—too deep to search for a body. We spent the next hour using a long extension pole with a hook on the end trying to retrieve all the plane debris from the water. The Coast Guard also assisted with their large vessel using a small crane onboard to pull up the heavier and larger pieces such as one half of a wing and the tail section. This would enable the appropriate experts to determine the cause of the crash.

Before we left the scene, I spent a minute just trying to take it all in. When I glanced over at the personal fishing boat, I noticed for the first time, a young boy. He was roughly the age of my son Cole. *Wow, what if he saw this?* It became obvious, that the military men on board didn't want to subject the boy to the same trauma they had experienced in combat, and had ordered the boy below deck. I know he had to have seen something… but what? I couldn't help but wonder, *how this will impact his life?*

Kellen and I were in a miserable funk on the boat ride back to the harbor. Although we didn't say much, we both agreed that death came quickly. We also compared what we saw of the victims, and realized that there had to have been tremendous force upon impact. We both wished we'd had a chance to help these people. This outcome was just another reminder that life wasn't predictable or fair, and we mourned for the family of the victims.

Waiting at the Harbor Patrol dock was a media circus which had encroached on the parking lots and sand. A fatality plane crash in North County San Diego was a rare occurrence, and they were all clamoring to report on the unfolding tragedy. The Coast Guard dock located on the west side of the harbor was surrounded by parked emergency vehicles. I noticed that there was a California State Lifeguard truck parked there as well; an agency not involved in the rescue or retrieval in this emergency.

Curious, I asked my lieutenant, "Why is a State Lifeguard truck here?" "Poor guy, you're not going to believe this. Of all planes to go down it was his in-laws. He was also scanning channel 16 when he heard the distress call. He knew this was about the same time his in-laws were taking off."

When I arrived home that evening, my wife Jen had prepared my favorite meal – steak. Enthusiastically, she greeted me at the door not knowing anything about my day, or what I had just experienced. She led me into the dining room to show me the beautiful table with all the trimmings waiting for me. I took one look at the steak, and I sighed. I gazed at Jen, and said "I'm sorry Honey, but I won't be able to eat meat tonight... or for awhile!" I grabbed the bottle of wine from the table, poured two hearty glasses, apologized profusely, and proceeded to tell her about my day.

Again, the worst part about tragedies such as this one is having to watch the family of the victims go through so much pain. It never gets easier... actually; it has probably gotten harder for me to watch.

CHAPTER 12

THE SHOVEL

"Man is worse than an animal, when he is an animal." ~
Rabindranath Tagore

This was neither the first nor the last time we had to deal with unsavory people at our beaches. There had been the time two ex-cons threatened to kill one lifeguard, and chased him down the pier. They were big, outlaw biker types with long, shaggy, greasy hair, wearing flannel shirts and filthy Levi's. One had a full beard and the other an oversized, cowboy-type mustache sitting above a mouth missing the left front tooth. I don't know exactly how the lifeguard set these two guys off, but they were hell-bent on putting the hurt on him. Luckily for the lifeguard, he simply climbed over the railing of the pier and jumped off, dropping about 40 feet into the ocean. The men were arrested at gunpoint and never seen again.

Then, there was the summer of 2002, where there were fights almost every day in just about every location on our beach. The parking lots, the sand, the park, and even in the water. There was one particular group of young males that were notorious in going around fighting anyone who'd look at them "wrong". One day, in front of 100 Jr. Lifeguards, they were chasing somebody and calling them every name in the book. One of our lifeguards Josh, approached the thugs, and told them to stop the profanity, and to get out of here. They yelled profanities at Josh and told him they were going to "get him!"

A few weeks later, after playing an evening game of

basketball, Josh, Mike, myself and a few other lifeguards went out for a couple beers at a local watering hole. As I was sipping on my beer, one of the guys I was with said, "Heads up, those are the guys that were giving Josh a hard time the other day." Their group outnumbered us 3-1. We were not looking for a fight but we'd never leave a brother unprotected. Josh knew he needed to get out of there. As he was headed out the back, 3 guys came out of nowhere, and jumped him. Josh managed to inflict several good hits on the perpetrators… then, all hell broke loose! Mike and I jumped in, and threw some "hay-makers," and we took a few shots as well. Two of our friends got Josh out and into their car. Mike, myself, and another guy went behind the bar, and armed ourselves with large schooners and told the bar tender to call the police… now! We held them off with verbal demands and threats of our own! We must have resembled wild animals being cornered. Their postures indicated to me that they were unsure now whether to continue this assault, or to high tail it out of there. The group dispersed before the cops arrived, and we explained what had happened the previous week. The next day, the Police Chief ordered officers to make contact with every member of the gang, and make them aware that if they had anymore run-ins with a lifeguard they would be arrested. The charges would be the same as assaulting a peace officer because this entire incident stemmed from an "on duty" situation.

Neal, by far had witnessed the most savage, and violent act. During one of his first years of lifeguarding he was walking up from our headquarters to a parking lot one block away from the beach. As he approached Pacific St., step by step he noticed a blue low-rider vehicle with 2 black males inside stop suddenly. The passenger jumped out, and quickly ran up behind a group of flashy, unruly males who looked like there were up to no good. The passenger pulled out from his waist band a nickel plated, semi-automatic handgun. Instantly, Neal saw 2 flashes as he simultaneously heard two popping sounds. Then he noticed one of the young men melt to the ground in a pool of blood. He had just witnessed somebody being assassinated.

One particular day lifeguarding, my partner Chase and I were taking a break at headquarters. We wanted to get out of the sun for a few minutes, drink some cold water, and let the air conditioner do its thing. As we sat in the meeting room extinguishing our thirst, in walked a thug who looked like he was on some sort of mission. About 5'10" tall and a few pounds over 200, this Hispanic male seemed to have tattoos from the top of his shaved head down to his feet. His long, white socks went all the way up his legs to his baggy shorts...typical dress code for a "cholo", or "homeboy." Most of the time, gang members didn't bother us. They were actually quite respectful. This guy, though, glared at us like a rabid animal before proceeding into the women's restroom. Chase and I looked at each other incredulously.

Suddenly remembering that there was a young female lifeguard in there, we hastily walked in after him. "Get the fuck out of here!" Chase yelled. Not knowing if he had a weapon or not, we tried to corral him toward the garage as soon as he came out.

We succeeded in getting him to walk out into the garage, but he suddenly stopped in his tracks. "You need to leave now." I told him.

"Make me," he responded defiantly as he continuously stared at me with dark, soulless eyes.

"L-10 for L-12, I need Code 3 backup at headquarters for a possible 5150," I uttered into the emergency radio.

The man appeared unfazed. "I said, make me, homes," Then he started to grab at his waistband.

Thinking he might be going for a weapon, I seized the closest thing to me, a shovel. As if fending off a grizzly with a big spear, I backed him up a few feet into our parking lot. The sounds of wailing sirens were now coming from all directions. "You grab your waistband or move towards me again, the pointy part of this shovel is going through your neck," I threatened.

Out of the corner of my eye, I noticed a lifeguard truck pulling up fast. The male started to put his hands near his waist again just as two figures sprinted in and absolutely blasted him over the two-foot retaining wall separating the parking lot from the sand.

Ryan and Blake! Perfect timing and the perfect guys for the job; Ryan stood six feet, weighed 215 pounds, played free safety for Oceanside High School, and was "used to" this sort of thing. Blake, a Samoan of 6'2", 220 pounds, stood by fuming with indignation. The two of them looked like a blitz package designed by Coach Pete Carroll.

Chase and I joined in, and we all jumped on this guy. Ryan took the perpetrator's face and shoved it into the sand, while Blake and I manipulated his arms to get him under control. "Damn, dude, my handcuffs are rusty," Blake said with a smirk.

We continued to wrestle with this crook constantly manipulating his arms and legs until there was no more fight left in him. His face was purple from being smothered into the sand. Ryan's knee applied the force to the back of his head.

Within minutes, the police showed up and arrested him. They seemed impressed because their only duty was to apply the handcuffs. The lifeguards packaged him up well. After running a check on him, it was discovered he had a history of assaulting police officers. They also found a 5 inch shank on him. The experience made me truly appreciate how lifeguards, police, and firefighters all look after each other. In beach towns, this is vital.

One day, when I was about 22, I was surfing on the south side of the pier. I accidentally dropped in on a local "Joe Pro Surfer", and he shot his board at me barely missing my head. As the wave broke we both collided in the white wash. As soon as he surfaced he raised both hands in the air and said, "Get out of here, go home kook." I responded with, "I'm sorry I didn't see you." He then proceeded to paddle right up to me, and attempted to punch me in the head. I blocked his fist with my arm that I stuck out to shield myself. Instinct kicked in as I got off my board, and started to egg beat my legs as if I were playing water polo. Not wanting to get in serious trouble I elevated my body above his. I came down on him pressing both of his shoulders down with my hands and my body on top of his head. I dunked him hard! He may be a way better surfer than me, but there is no way he is going to get the better of me in a fight in the water! As I allowed him to surface he had a look of, I'm going to get you back on his face, but he also realized the gravity of the situation. "You're the one who needs to go home," I said, as I started to paddle out again. "You will never surf here again" he screamed out at me.

My friends and brother Neal were looking on as they heard all the yelling. I relayed to them that the "Joe Pro Surfer" tried to punch me, and how I responded. Just then my friend Thorsten said, "Hey Dave is that the guy paddling this way with Junior?" *Ah hell,* I thought. Junior was a 300 pound Samoan long boarder who paddled right towards me. "Hey, did you assault my little friend here bro?" Mentally, I was rattled as I tried to hold my position even though every thought said paddle to shore. "He needs to show respect Junior" I said, as I sat up on my board. "He tried to punch me, and I dunked him. Shouldn't he fight his own battles?" As I continued, my brother, and 3 other off duty lifeguards circled around Junior. "Junior, I respect you, and would never throw a

punch at you. Your boy did, he's lucky I didn't really hurt him."
Amazingly, Junior looked around, assessed the situation, threw his
hands in the air and said, "Fuck it, let's all surf!" A few months
later we found out that Junior's dad died. Our whole staff sent his
family flowers, a sympathy card, and our captain even went to the
funeral. This touched him deeply. Since that day, he often comes
by headquarters to see how we are all doing.

CHAPTER 13

NEAL: LIFEGUARDING VS. FIREFIGHTING

I began my longstanding lifeguarding career in the summer of 1987, during my sophomore year in high school. It was not by accident or chance. The "water folk" of our coastal communities are born and bred through generations of civic duty, and a dedication to athleticism in the water. My family has a solid history of involvement with public service; including my father and two brother's employment as lifeguards during their young adulthood. So it was that coincidence had nothing to do with my eventual matriculation into the world of beach guarding. My twin brother Dave was hired the same year as me.

I was lucky enough to have attended Oceanside High School, the older, and more ideal of the city's two public high schools in terms of its proximity to the coveted sands of the local beaches... no small privilege when you're young, money poor, and stricken with that kind of boundless energy only experienced in youth. It was *great* to be a teenager in "O'side" in those days!

The preparation for this calling began several months before trying out for the job. I obtained certification in the various academic fundamentals required of every lifeguard. Include were CPR, first aid, and water safety training… all of this *before* the most daunting task of surviving the rigorous tryout, and demonstration protocol mandated by the City of Oceanside Lifeguards. Oceanside is famous for its wide, sandy-white beaches; an inarguable blessing which our neighbors to the south in Carlsbad have long envied. The attendance on our beaches is vastly higher than on other local beaches, in turn demanding an extraordinarily capable and competitive lifeguarding force. To be a beach guard in Oceanside was and still is a very coveted spot to win. I was young, motivated, fortunate, and admittedly a little full of myself, as were most of my peers.

In truth, my preparation had begun years earlier, when I discovered my love of water. I would spend hours upon hours in the pools of Oceanside, and the waves of local waters, perfecting my aquatic skills along the way. I do want to make clear that even though someone may be a gifted pool swimmer, he or she is not automatically qualified as an ideal beach guard candidate. Anyone with substantial ocean swimming experience knows they must anticipate the sea's wild mood swings, and be aware of the fragility of the human body compared to its powerful capacity.

The other prevailing factor besides the physical requirements of the job of lifeguarding is the simple fact that human beings are either natural responders, or natural bystanders. All the training in the world will not counteract this one human inclination. The human element that predisposes one to civil service—or doesn't— can't be discounted no matter how qualified someone might be in and around the water. Even though I consider myself to have an inordinate amount of ocean experience; my longevity in the career is basically owing to my "people skills." The variability of the human response either as rescuer or victim was the biggest hurdle in my duties as a lifeguard, and later as a firefighter.

Lifeguarding was essentially a great springboard for my eventual career in the fire service. In the spring of 1999, I was fortunate to earn a position as a firefighter/paramedic with the City of San Marcos, which is further inland and just north of my stomping grounds in Oceanside, but still part of North San Diego County. Having worked as a fire medic for over 15 years, I have become well-versed in the intrinsic similarities between my two professions, as well as how my lifeguarding job absolutely cultivated my move to fire service.

As I reflect, there are as many differences as there are similarities between lifeguarding and firefighting. At its core, the fire service is a *reactive* response profession, while many of my duties on the beach involved *preventative* measures. Firefighters are generally waiting to respond to calls, so regardless of whether you're training, studying, eating, or sleeping when the alarm sounds you're at the whim of luck and circumstance. Once the call comes in, there is a great deal of variety as to the nature of the incident, which leads to never being bored, and a better overall honing of your acquired skill set. As a firefighter, I'm acquainted with every type of catastrophe, from a brush fire to domestic violence. The diversity of situations encountered mandates ongoing advanced training and continuing education. With the exception of water rescues, firefighters are the ones who ultimately arrive to mitigate a disaster. But, no one scene of calamity is totally predictable, so, the services rendered cover a multitude of medical and procedural demands.

The fire service is inherently better at taking control of large-scale incidents. I believe this is due to the advanced age, and training of fire personnel compared to lifeguards. In fire service, there is simply more experience regarding the Incident Command System than exists among the lifeguarding chain of command. The bigger the incident, the greater is the need to efficiently coordinate the efforts of multiple responding agencies. Identifying and utilizing all the available resources is often the first and greatest predicament to overcome when on a multi-agency call. Landing helicopters, asking for additional fire apparatus, contacting hospitals with multiple casualties, or ordering a Hazardous Materials Team (HAZMAT) are all vital components of scene management and administration of a basic standard of care. For this reason, most hours accumulated in the fire service are spent taking classes, training on new equipment, and learning the newest and most efficient way to extricate a patient from a mangled car.

The fire service is constantly evolving through trial and error to effectively respond to any and all emergency situations.

Life in fire service is also unique given the living quarters for personnel. The social aspect of the job is probably the most comical and entertaining component of it. Everything you can imagine happens under the roof of a firehouse! In fact, I think a sociologist could easily write a bestseller if he or she went from firehouse to firehouse in this country, and documented the wide range of unorthodox behavior going on. What else could be expected in a "home" that encompasses every age group and demographic, but with each resident individualistic, alpha dominant, and in possession of a strong personality? Throwing a bunch of people with these characteristics together under one roof is an explosive mixture of humor, hostility, ego, cliques, and endless practical jokes. Most of us are husbands and fathers with normal life stressors, and coupled with the pressures of firefighting, there are bound to be some "touchy" moments. I learned very quickly the quirks and ticks of my "work family," and as happens in most families, you learn how to build each other up, or quickly tear each other down. The result is everything from harmless bantering to strategically mastered pranks... like the time a rainbow flag bumper sticker was put on the truck of a homophobic firefighter, who retaliated by putting a bag of oregano under the bumper of a guy who routinely goes through a Border Patrol checkpoint on his way home from work. All in the name of brotherly love! Although I have never seen any fistfights in my department, there have been some long-term "cold wars," i.e. hostility between peers who have had a falling out. Usually, it works itself out. All this aside, I can state without doubt that none of us would hesitate to risk his life to save a fellow firefighter.

The job of ocean lifeguarding is a different animal altogether. Just as I discussed how fire service involves reactivity; the primary function of a lifeguard is to be *proactive*. Lifeguards strive to prevent dangerous situations in and around the water, but if something out of the ordinary occurs, they need to observe it, and react accordingly. Considering this, lifeguards are some of the best—much like law enforcement—at sizing people up, and predicting what they might do next. Despite our society's focus on "political correctness," lifeguards use every stereotype in the world to gauge how people might interact with each other, and the ocean. You wouldn't let an "international traveler" from south of the border swim next to the pier pilings in a south swell in his cut-off Levi's, would you? Would you let a drunk "redneck" from the Inland Empire wearing surf trunks with a wife-beater tee shirt, surf inshore breakers alongside hundreds of young swimmers? Of course not!! When I see one group of gangsters walking towards another group of gangsters, I'm instantly going to get the police rolling down to that location. Racial profiling? Maybe, but I can't say that I care. You may hate the method, but you can't understate its practicality in preventing the worst.

I think you get the picture on why it's important to be proactive as a beach guard. Your head is constantly swiveling as you assess and discard every potential hazard existing in and out of the water. The people on land are every bit as volatile as the condition of the surf at any given time. If you catch yourself daydreaming, you must mentally check yourself, or rotate out and off-duty. Are the weak swimmers being caught by an identifiable rip current? Is that three-year-old lost? Did that body boarder surface after that last set of waves? It is a never-ending parade of checks and balances.

Unlike firefighters, who always respond as a cohesive team, lifeguards mostly act individually. This can be unsettling at times. For instance, if you are patrolling the beach by yourself in midwinter, and you witness a boat capsize in unusually large surf while navigating into the harbor; you're temporarily on your own as the first responder. After you radio in for backup, you are acting alone for a good five to ten minutes before additional help arrives. There are many times a lifeguard has to act alone during tough situations, relying on their individual problem-solving skills, and physical capability to get through them.

Both firefighting and lifeguarding can be very physically demanding at times. Fighting structure fires and wildfires on land in extreme conditions can push anybody to the limit. For a lifeguard, the requirements of regular exposure to the elements, running and swimming for several hours each day, relegate this job to a young person. You are also the ambassador for the city in which you work, approachable by anyone and everyone. "Hey, lifeguard, where can I swim? Where can I surf? Where can I rent a bike? Where's a good restaurant? Are there sharks in the water?" The questions go on and on and on! Many lifeguards who are reading this book can probably relate to waking up in the middle of the night, finding their eyes transfixed on the wall, as if it's the section of water they're guarding.

Some of the questions, though, I appreciated! "Do you have a girlfriend? Can I have your number?" There's nothing like being young, male, and surrounded by women in bikinis. It's long days, and even longer nights with the ladies. This is another reason that lifeguarding is a young man's job... or maybe a better term is "sport."

Despite the physical demands of lifeguarding, and the fact that your brain has turned to mush by the end of the day, the body doesn't necessarily slow down after sunset. The social aspect of lifeguarding is, in my opinion, second to none. Whereas in firefighting, your peers are men and women you've never met before, in lifeguarding you're paired with guys and girls with whom you grew up swimming, and playing water polo. Bonds have already been long established, and now you're testing the waters on more than one front. It's definitely a closely knit, family-like environment, as well as a revolving door of incestuous in-dating among peers and friends. Did I mention the lifeguard parties? They're the perfect environment for healthy, good-looking people to get together after-hours; sand still in their toes, beers in their hands, and their loved ones sitting on their laps. The stories! Oh man... the stories!

During my years of lifeguarding, there were countless parties one could attend. They happened almost every night after work ranging from small group gatherings at someone's house to the annual rookie party. Rookie parties were notorious for being wild—a night when the rookie lifeguards paid for a huge feast, booze, and catered to the more senior guards. After the lifeguards were fat and happy, their friends would show up. There'd be upwards of 200 people at rookie parties. They were usually held at a house with a swimming pool, where lifeguards were quick to shed their gear, and jump into the pool or Jacuzzi. After that, things could get very foggy; you might find yourself the next morning under a eucalyptus tree all dirty, smelling like old beer, lying next to a good-looking girl who works as a dolphin trainer at Sea World.

The annual Oceanside Body Surfing Contest, held in mid-August. The community center right next to lifeguard headquarters is where the dance/party took place. If my memory serves me right, it was always the girls from Santa Cruz who would strip down naked, run across The Strand, and make their way into the water. To them, Oceanside's water felt like a Jacuzzi compared to the frigid water of Santa Cruz. Sooner or later, all the dudes would take off their clothes, and chase after them like a Benny Hill comedy. It was a complete spectacle to see all these guys and girls wrestling around in the water, and ending up on the sand making out like a bunch of human grunions.

All in all, both lifeguarding and firefighting were and are character-building professions. I do not feel that one is "better," but rather I believe that these professions complement each other. It's a natural progression from lifeguard to firefighter, if one chooses that path. I also have the utmost respect for lifeguards who choose to make that their permanent career. Who knows? Maybe when I retire from the fire service, I'll return to lifeguarding... if I can withstand the dreaded re-qualification swim when I'm in my 50's. Man, those winter re-quals f—ing hurt!

CHAPTER 14

ENDURANCE ABOVE ALL

"Lifeguarding in its purest form is the struggle against nature by one human endeavoring to save the life of another." ~ Unknown (written on the wall inside Oceanside Lifeguard Headquarters)

As I walked my beach cruiser up to the house I took off my back pack and stretched out my arm to punch in the code for the garage door. *My arms feel heavy*, I thought, as I rolled my bike into its space against the inside wall. Sweat that accumulated under my baseball cap from the ride home now gushed down over my face as I removed it. I peeled off my saturated shirt, wiped my face, and immediately tossed it on the ground. As I walked into the house my wife greets me in the kitchen. She did one of those elevator looks, her eyes gazed me up and down. Shocked by my appearance she asks "Where have you been all day, the gym? Your biceps are bulging, you look like The Rock!" "Sit down," I told her. "Do I have a story for you!" I chugged a beer to take the edge off and said, "I think I just made the rescue of my career."

The last two hours of a ten-hour shift seem to last forever, but this is only part of why we refer to them as the "lifeguard witching hours." It was late June in 2014, and even though it was almost 6:00 p.m., the beach crowd was still thick. Both the air and water temperatures were hovering around 75 degrees. It was the type of evening when beach-lovers languished in the water until the sun went down. My partner Shay and I had decided to take one last beach run in the lifeguard truck, a trek of about a mile-and-a-half past the Oceanside Pier to the north jetty at the Harbor beach. This would take approximately 20 minutes—just enough time to get back to headquarters, wash up, and call it a day.

Shay had recently graduated from UC Santa Barbara and was planning a career working for the U.S. government in some capacity or another. She was a few months shy of entering Officer Candidate School at the coastguard academy in Connecticut. Even though her world views were somewhat different for my taste, when it came to the water, I knew Shay could more than hold her own. She was the epitome of Southern California beach lifeguard at six feet tall, with long, sandy-blonde hair and glowing skin. More importantly, she was a solid guard.

We were approaching Tower 6 when Shay noticed that the lifeguard there had her binoculars focused on something in the water. "Dave, pull up to the tower," she directed me. "Let's see why she seems so frazzled with intensity."

As we pulled up alongside the tower, the guard suddenly threw off her jacket, grabbed her can and fins, and sprinted towards the water. As I exited the truck, I noticed the massive dust trail she had just kicked up. *She never runs this hard...this must be serious!* I thought. I balanced myself on the rail step of our yellow Nissan Frontier to get a better view of what was going on in the water. About 40 yards north of Tower 6, the water churned brown and frothy in the telltale sign of a rip current. This was no typical rip current though, it looked to be about the size of two football fields lined up end to end, including their width. It was a river of water being sucked out to sea. Five heads bobbed inside it, calling for help and frantically trying to get their exhausted arms above the surface of the water.

"Shay, call for more guards before heading out," I yelled as I reached for my can and fins. Since the victims were in such bad shape, out about 150 yards, and all separated from one another, I feared this emergency was going to escalate into a body search instead of a call for distressed swimmers.

Sprinting 60 yards in soft sand had already elevated my heart rate, and now I had to run and jump through shallow water until I could begin the swimming part of the rescue. The long-shore lateral current was cranking to the north because of a modest southwest swell that was hitting our beach, so I made sure to enter the water well south of the victims, anticipating the likely drift. My blue-and-black "duck feet" swim fins were gripped firmly in my left hand, my red "Pete Peterson" can in my right. Once in ankle-deep water, I threw the can forward. It was still held by a strap around my chest. In one motion, I pulled the strap up over my head and repositioned it over my left shoulder and opposite armpit. As I continued high-step running through the water, I rotated one of my fins into my now-free right hand and then dove dolphin-style into the water when it was above my knees. Once I was deep enough to start swimming, I dipped under a wave while putting my fins on. Then I popped up and swam freestyle, my head above the surface, as fast as I could towards the group in trouble. These are the basic maneuvers I have used countless times, from my very first rescue to the ones I perform now.

The waves were running three to five feet, which was nothing I normally couldn't handle and not unusual for our beaches. They were, however, coming in very consistently and breaking top to bottom, which gave them tremendous power. Since the wave pitches, the water is thrown on top of you, with heavy pounding force. Bottom line—it made for an exhausting swim because it was relentless, and never giving me a break in between sets. Otherwise, I could easily swim out there uncontested, but with every wave it was a constant thrashing. If I stopped swimming, I would lose ground and would end up swimming more distance. The two victims closest to shore were already canned and safely being swam to shore by the first responding tower guard. They were young teenage girls who were grateful for having been safely returned to shore. Knowing there were more rescues out there, I kept pushing toward the other heads. After another half-minute of all-out power swimming, I came upon two more girls doing a cross between a breast stroke and doggie paddle. They were both hysterically crying, and their wet hair draped across their faces and snot running down their noses. They absolutely did not care about their appearance, though, because unbeknownst to me, they had just drifted past the floating but unmoving body of their friend. Once I made eye contact with one of the girls, she screamed in anguish, "Our friend is way out there and he drowned!!" "Where is he?" I yelled. They frantically pointed out towards the horizon. As I looked out I saw a black dot bobbing 60 yards out where the biggest waves were breaking. *You can't be serious,* I thought. I'm already exhausted, but my adrenaline kicked in. As I looked out one more time I noticed another batch of these menacing waves. There is absolutely no choice, I put my head down into the water and started engaging in this battle against nature for the life of this boy.

I felt reassured leaving the girls to Shay and the tower guard, who were not far behind me. If I delayed any longer, there might be no hope for the fifth and possibly drowned victim. He was on the cusp of being outside the breaking waves, but still in the impact zone of the biggest sets.

It dawned on me as I put my head down to swim that I was the only thing in the world that could save this boy's life. There was no WaveRunner, boat, surfer, or other lifeguard...JUST ME! I was one of the oldest guards on staff and fortunately for the victim, the most experienced. Nonetheless, swim-sprinting through the relentless surf was taking its toll on my body, similarly aged with my longevity as a lifeguard and I began feeling bogged down with fatigue. One of the many thoughts were flashing through my brain as I kept hammering through this swim, was "life and death" wasn't just a dramatic expression, but a reality for that boy floating out there. Rather than encourage me, however, my brain started questioning my motives for still being a guard after nearly 30 years. The mental torture went something like, *if he drowns and I lose him, I'm done! Who am I kidding! I'll tear my patch off of my shorts, hand it to my captain and tell him I'm quitting! I'm too old for this job!* As I dove under another wave, I pop my head up to get a visual of the victim and I continue to think, *I have to get him…not only does he die, but his mom and family will be crushed, forever brokenhearted. What if he were my son? I would never forgive myself!* Even though we are rigorously trained to be lifeguards, we are still very human and experience things personally, right along with our victims.

I was closing in on the boy, who now resembled a random floating object more than a human being struggling for life. I didn't dare take my eyes off his very still form. I was only ten yards away and I saw the boy try to raise his arms above his head as he quietly sunk below the surface of the water. *He just gave up. Are you f-ing kidding me this is not going to happen on my watch! Not now after all this!* I just witnessed a passive drowning. I have one shot to locate and pull him up. Opening my eyes under water I realize I can't see my hand in front of my face. The water was beyond murky. *How the hell am I going to find this kid? Just dive down Wags in the direction you last saw him.* As I forced the last bit of energy I had left in my body, I took a deep breath and followed my last stroke under water. My fins made a vigorous splash as they propelled me downward. With my arms stretched out in front of me, I blindly sank my hands into the top of his shoulders. I grabbed him across the chest and under the arms, and we start our journey to the surface. Our bodies broke through the surface of the water as I shouted out from complete body fatigue and agony, "I got you! I got you! I got you!"

As I wrapped the red lifeguard buoy around his waist, he spoke in a barely audible whisper. "Thank you... thank you...thank you."

I clipped the victim and secured him like a big game fish that couldn't get away. "What is your name?" I asked.

"Kevin."

"Well, Kevin, you and I are going to float here for a few minutes while we both catch our breath". He was very pale, and his lips had an unnatural bluish tint to them which is associated with cyanosis. He was also throwing up a lot, indicating that it was likely he had water in his lungs.

Shay popped out the back of a wave and proceeded to swim up to us. "All four girls are safely on shore. Do you need help?"

"Kevin is going to need medical attention," I responded. Shay looked towards shore and began pumping her fist up and down trying to get the attention of the lifeguard who was now in the tower. The tower guard made a big "O" with his arms above his head, signaling "okay." Two other lifeguard trucks had responded Code 3 – "lights and sirens" – to our location. As we brought Kevin to the waterline, other guards were making more rescues in the same rip. Two other responding lifeguards were waiting for us at one of the trucks, with oxygen ready. As Kevin began receiving oxygen through a mask, one of the lifeguards placed a stethoscope to his back and instructed him to take a deep breath. When a victim takes a deep breath, the lifeguard listens for any crackling noise which signifies there is water in the lungs. Many near-drowning victims forgo continued medical treatment, but then succumb to drowning on land because their lungs were never cleared.

When the paramedics arrived, they took over patient management, including more testing for lung sounds to determine if Kevin had aspirated any seawater. Like us, they were intent on avoiding a "parking lot" or secondary drowning from lungs retaining seawater. Salt in the lungs can cause a build-up of fluids, resulting in pulmonary edema. I have witnessed near drownings where the victim vomits up pink, frothy sputum that resembles Pepto-Bismol®. This is a symptom of pulmonary edema, and in my experience, it doesn't take long to develop. Kevin's lungs were determined to be clear and because he was a minor, the paramedics notified his parents before they were legally permitted to release him.

Reflecting on this incident, I concluded that Kevin had passed the stage of actively drowning, characterized by the victim struggling and screaming at the surface of the water. By the time I was able to reach him, Kevin had mentally and physically conceded his life. Some call this stage "making peace with God," although lifeguards refer to it as the passive drowning mechanism. This boy's rescue once again reinforced the need for surf rescue lifeguards to be in excellent physical shape, regardless of years spent on the beach and in uniform. The mandate to pass a rigorous physical re-qualification test every year is—and should always be—the priority in maintaining a superior rescue force for Oceanside's beaches. Lifeguarding is not just about being brave, but being able to endure and not quit.

The next morning, as I walked into Lifeguard Headquarters, Jason who is a 6 year guard said, "Great rescue yesterday, I was watching you from pier tower with high powered binoculars." "At first, I didn't know where you were swimming to." "Thanks! Did I look slow and tired?" "No, I thought you were Austin." (Austin is the fastest swimmer on our staff – he's in his early 20's) Then he chuckled and said, "You've still got it old man!"

The following Spring to my surprise, I opened an email from Lt. Blake Faumuina. I was informed that not only had I been secretly nominated, but I had been awarded, the *Medal of Valor* for this rescue. I felt deeply proud and genuinely honored. The ceremony was heartwarming to me because many of my colleagues, friends and my family showed up to share this honor with me.

CHAPTER 15

THE PADDLE OUT

"Sometimes you will never know the true value of a moment until it becomes a memory." ~ Iman - wife of David Bowie

When a young, vibrant boy unexpectedly dies in an accident, it grips the community in collective shock and pain. People from all different walks of life seek each other out in mutual heartbreak, looking for answers and comfort from others who, many times, they have never even met. The passing of such a fresh and innocent soul makes people reflect not only on their own lives, but on the lives of the people they love. It is even harder for those who can identify with the victim or family bearing such a huge loss.

In late October of 2015, the city of Oceanside experienced such a tragedy when a middle-school-aged boy riding his bike to school was hit by a truck. The child, an aspiring surfer loved by a great number of friends and family, had been riding down a hill facing traffic in the bike lane. He was clipped, and then crushed by the vehicle of an elderly driver who had no clue he was there. Some of the firefighters on the scene were visibly crying. Working as a firefighter or paramedic and running calls involving kids is a nightmare, and every parent's worst fear is getting that phone call...

Word of this accident spread fast, as did the grief of all who had known him. Among those devastated were his school friends, soccer teammates, fellow junior lifeguards, and even people who were simply acquainted with him or his family. To honor this young man's life, it was decided by family and friends that they would do a "paddle out." This is a ceremony during which mourners paddle out into the ocean, past the breakers, on surfboards or boats. They come together in a circle in the calmer water past the surf to share stories, hold hands, and pray for the person who has passed. Often, flowers and/or the decedent's ashes are spread on the water, as everyone splashes or cheers in a final celebration of that person's life. It was an appropriate way to commemorate this young man's adventurous soul and love of the ocean. Most importantly, it would bring everyone together to share their common sorrow and hopefully begin healing.

When I reported to work the Sunday after the accident, I was told we would be lifeguarding a huge paddle out in his honor. It was a beautiful, sunny day, and the water was warm, but there was one problem: the surf was six to seven feet and breaking top to bottom with a lot of force. My mind was racing. *Did we have enough lifeguards on duty? Who was in charge of the paddle out?* This could go sideways really quick, and we had to be as prepared as possible. All hands were on deck, and in the end, we mustered up as many lifeguards as we could, given our short notice of the event. There were about 12 of us for approximately 400 paddlers, which was not a huge presence…but these were very good watermen, ready to give their condolences as well as their watchful eyes. Half of the paddlers were kids aged 10 to 12, which was again a bad recipe in terms of potential for danger in the water.

Standing by our paddle-boards, we lifeguards made small talk as we shifted our feet in the sand. It had been agreed that we would all wear fins, just in case we got overwhelmed with victims and lost our boards. Prayers and directions for the paddle out were given over a loudspeaker by a family member, who urged everyone to be as cautious as possible. One of our sergeants suggested staggering the paddlers into heats so there wouldn't be boards flying into other paddlers. However, because it wasn't an officially sanctioned City of Oceanside event, we had to limit our involvement and coordinating efforts. All we could really do was give them a lot of suggestions.

The first paddlers were quickly swept up the beach by a powerful southern swell, and by the time they made it past the surf, they were 100 yards to the north of the designated meeting spot. The following heats moved far enough south before starting their trek to compensate for the current and swell. Fortunately, most of them gauged it pretty accurately.

The lifeguards also split into teams before we embarked on our own journey through the waves. I decided to run up the beach with six other guys to look after the first group of paddlers. I was amazed to see a little Hispanic girl—she couldn't have been more than 10 or 11 years old—trying to make it past the breakers wearing a hooded sweatshirt and pants. First, I felt angry. *No way…where were her parents?* But, this was immediately replaced by admiration. *Bless her heart! She doesn't want to miss out on celebrating her classmate's life. She gets an "A" for effort!* I could see, though, that she was getting tired and starting to succumb to the ocean. I paddled towards her from the west, and she was surprised when I suddenly appeared beside her. I immediately got her on my paddle-board lying prone and facing the nose of the board. I spotted a little three-foot wave, already broken, and gave her a nice ride back to shore.

After safely delivering the girl and getting a hug, I headed back out towards a group of paddlers on the verge of making it beyond the breakers. They were all Oceanside Junior Lifeguards who looked like they were having some fun with the challenge of getting to the ceremony despite being tumbled about by the pounding surf. I noticed a familiar face among the group who seemed to be watching the others and recognized Sunny Garcia, a former world champion surfer. Sunny lived in the area and had been contacted by a friend of the boy, who had told Sunny about the youth's tragic death, in addition to the fact that he had been the boy's idol. I know Sunny Garcia has a reputation for his temper and not being the nicest guy in the world, but this gesture struck a chord in me, and I thought this was a classy move on his part. I didn't make a big deal out of his being there, but gave him a simple nod of the head to hopefully convey that I thought highly of him for giving a damn.

Once everybody was safely outside the waves and gathered in a big circle, it was now emotions, not waves, that rose high. The boy's younger sister and mom were looking on from the Harbor Patrol boat while the dad was in the middle of the circle on his surfboard. A lot of friends and family members shared touching tributes. Then, it was time for the father to talk. This had been his only boy. *How are you being so strong?* I wondered. Unsurprisingly, the father did begin to break down, affecting each one of us. As a father myself, torturous questions popped into my mind. *How does he get up in the morning? How do you feel that empty void where there used to be a young soul, so eager to take on the world?* I could only conclude, *He is in a nightmare, with pain in his heart which will never go away.* As the ceremony ended, flowers were thrown and chants recited. The circle silently—almost eerily—broke up, and paddlers started to make their way back to shore.

Heading back in, the group did not bother separating into heats, which I knew was bound to result in problems. When the bulk of the 400 seagoing mourners entered the surf zone, the biggest set of the day was closing in on them. *No!* I thought. *This would be like the Daytona 500, except with surfboards flying everywhere!* Nearby was a dad with two young kids, and I decided to escort them as they paddled in…in these conditions and with the number of people in the water, I knew this little group stood a good chance of being pulverized.

The first wave knocked scores of people off their boards, which soared in all directions. I just hoped they didn't land on anyone's head! Panic set in as one of the boys in the triplet I was chaperoning started to yell for help. I grabbed his tiny waist with my left arm as I held onto the paddle-board with the other. "Take a deep breath, count to ten, and relax," I told him. One of the biggest waves of the day proceeded to break right on top of us. We tumbled and were slammed around violently, but I lived up to my promise that I would not let him go. My right hand gripped the handle of the paddle-board as it was violently thrown towards shore. Before surfacing I felt a ping and an easing of pressure on my right ring finger. *I wouldn't be surprised if I just lost my fingertip*, I sensed grimly.

When our heads were above water, the little boy yelled "Ewww!" I knew what he was looking at, but didn't want to look myself. Finally, I glanced at my right hand and saw the finger flopped over, dangling by a thin strip tissue. The broken ends each had a small bone jutting out. I elevated my hand out of the water and held onto the boy.

When there was a lull in the surf, I started to wave towards shore in hopes of getting another lifeguard on the beach to assist me. Luckily, the dad and other boy washed into us, headed towards shore. "Hey, I got my son. Go take care of your finger," he yelled.

I clamped down with my left hand, securing my right ring finger while I kicked towards shore. Once I had managed to get to waist deep water, two lifeguards ran over. One passed me and swam out to secure the group I had been with. The other walked me up to the lifeguard truck and made sure I was going to get medical attention.

There to help me out was a lifeguard named Kaipo, who also worked as a paramedic in San Diego. Also, with him was an Oceanside firefighter. "Wrap it up nicely," I told them. "I don't want to lose it."

They were calm, cool, and collected. Kaipo smirked at me. "Take a deep breath and count to ten, big boy," he joked, and we both laughed. As they wrapped up my finger and hand, the father and boys from the paddle back into shore approached us, along with the mother. She walked right up to me, gave me a hug, and said, "How's the finger?"

I spent the next eight hours in the emergency room getting my finger sewn back on. To this day, it still sticks out funny, but at least I still have it. Reflecting back on it all, I know the situation could've been much worse. Overall, 46 rescues were performed in that short period of time the swimmers were journeying back to shore after the paddle out. I think most of us at that day's event felt a new appreciation for life, for a few reasons. The underlying feeling among the group reminded me of the community spirit I sense in my city of Oceanside. Since we are all struggling at times to make our way through life, maybe the best thing to do is love everyone like family. Imagine the world if *all* people were in harmony and cared about each other? The day of the paddle out, I felt very conscious of this atmosphere of love and togetherness, so despite what happened to my finger, I am deeply grateful I could be part of it.

CHAPTER 16

NO CHANCE

"Sorrow looks back
Worry looks around
Faith looks up"

~Ralph Waldo Emerson

January 22ⁿᵈ, 2017

The heavy rain drenched me as I ran from my parked car into Lifeguard Headquarters. Although it's only eight 'o clock in the morning, there was already a buzz of anxious energy inside. The handfuls of lifeguards already on duty were busy organizing their swift water rescue gear. Dry suites, booties, gloves, helmets, flashlights, knifes, ropes, personal flotation devises (PFD'S), and various hardware was being packed into large travel bags. Unlike the, "high incident, low risk" ocean rescues we performed daily, swift water rescues were rare, but looking like a real possibility today. These were "low incident, high risk" so; everyone wanted to be well prepared and ready on a moment's notice.

At 10:00am, LT. Faumuina herded all of us into the staff meeting room for our daily briefing. He advised, "Make sure you guys go over knot tying and rigging systems. We are expecting local flooding." He proceeded to put us into three teams of three. He told us we could be responding all over North County San Diego for mutual aid on water rescues. I was assigned with sergeants Tyler and Mason on team one.

Tyler was a former high school football player, who at 6'3 215 lbs., he was a force to be reckoned with! His blonde hair and blue eyes made him look like a stereo-typical southern California beach lifeguard. Although he can be very serious, and at times, have a no-nonsense personality at work, he always managed a smile. Tyler is one of the hardest working lifeguards on staff. He is very dedicated to being in top physical shape, as well as constantly evolving his technical lifeguard skills. He is constantly training in the fields of boat operations, EMT, diving, and swift water rescue. Mason, in my opinion, is one of the best athletes we have in our lifeguard brotherhood. He is not the biggest guy, but pound for pound one of the strongest. If you work out with him be prepared for a world of hurt! Whatever he dedicates himself to, he excels at. Surfing, cycling, and swimming are just a few. Mason is very sarcastic, and has a wise crack for everything and everybody. However, he has a big heart, and is easy to talk to. Both, Tyler and Mason have spent numerous hours swift water rescue training (SRT) in rivers in Northern California. I knew I was in good hands.

As I looked out the window of headquarters, I became mesmerized by the massive black clouds that were approaching from the north. It seemed like it never rained anymore in San Diego. I was awestruck. We have been in a severe drought since 2012. The last few years were the hottest on record and the 11th driest of all time. There were a couple of days that wildfires were burning in Carlsbad, San Marcos, and Oceanside, and all fire apparatus in our city were exhausted. It was so dire that they sent lifeguard trucks along with ambulances on medical calls throughout the city. There were literally no more engines. Hopefully, this storm will put a big dent into our drought.

After several hours of watching and waiting, Tyler and Mason wanted to go survey the San Luis Rey River. The three of us packed our belongings into the lifeguard truck and headed out. We drove down the trail that paralleled the river. Mason pointed out that there were actually rapids forming in places where the day before had no water. There were heaps of thick overgrown brushes that the water flowed into. All the dead trees from the drought that had fallen were now clogging up the flow of water. It resembled beaver damns everywhere. Tyler noted places to avoid, as well as good entry and exit points should there be an emergency.

As the sun started to set, we completed our river run. We headed back to Lifeguard Headquarters for the last couple hours of our shift. As we walked in, we hear our lieutenant informing the crew, "Since this morning, we've had 2 inches of rain locally on the coast, and much more inland. Brace yourselves; we could be in for a long night if this keeps up!" We all sat around the meeting room watching the Weather Channel, and inhaling our food because we were starving. Of course, you guessed it…burritos! While eating, we also talked about different possible scenarios we could be called on and how we would go about handling them. As I took my red salsa, and poured it down the crevices of my carne asada and potato (California) burrito, I heard the familiar sound. Beep! Beep! Beep! Our emergency radio pulsated throughout the room. North-Com was dispatching North County Firefighters for a water rescue in Rainbow. Rainbow is a small town in North East San Diego County right off the I-15 freeway. It is a small community full of nurseries that specialized in various palm trees and exotic plants. It is also known for its "green gold" avocados and marijuana. The area was also very susceptible to flooding because of the lack of adequate drainage systems.

"Team One get ready!" Lt. Faumuina barked. We all rolled out our dry suites and climbed into them. We were getting the rest of the gear together when another call came over North-Com requesting Oceanside Lifeguards.

Tyler, Mason, and I loaded our personal gear into the cab.

The technical equipment, rigging systems, and inflatable boat were all neatly organized in the bed of the truck. We headed east on Highway 76 towards Rainbow. Although we were driving, "code three" with our lights and sirens on, Mason was cautious knowing that there were flat low lying flooded areas on the highway. If not careful, it could make us hydroplane and flip the truck. Also, with the rain pouring down the visibility was limited, and very sketchy.

Tyler was riding in the passenger seat as he navigated, and monitored all radio traffic. Over the radio we heard, "Young boy reported in flooded creek. Nearby neighbors reported hearing and seeing a boy was being swept downstream, screaming for help." Tyler said, "You all hear that? Boy reported in flooded creek!" "We all heard it alright!" We all have kids of our own. Needless to say our intensity level went up several notches.

It was by far the longest drive out to an emergency call I have ever been on. My thoughts went back to the SRT class we did the previous winter in response to a growing El Nino. El Nino means warmer ocean water with that more rain. Rivers and swift water scare me more than the ocean. Both you can read and judge, but swift water has a lot more hazards especially during tremendous downfall. Unlike the ocean that has lulls in between sets of waves, swift water is constantly moving. If you step in the wrong place, your foot or leg can become entrapped. Who knows what is also flowing down stream. It could be a tree, refrigerator, or automobile. The most horrific things are strainers. Just like spaghetti strainers, things like fences, trees, bushes, vehicles, bridges, and other trappings will allow water to pass under and through it, thus strain larger objects. Think of it this way, water weighs 62 pounds per cubic foot, and then multiply by how deep the water is and times that again by how fast the water is moving. There is some type of mathematical formula I learned in my SRT class, but the bottom line is the force will be hundreds if not thousands of pounds. Word to the wise, avoid them! Once you are caught in one the likelihood of death is high. No matter how strong a person is, or how good of a swimmer you may be, there is usually no getting out of these death traps. You ultimately will drown from the pressure of the water holding you under.

There was no doubt in my mind that either Tyler or Mason will end up quarter backing this operation by the end of the night. They will do the technical planning. No way will they put their trust in anybody else. I just wanted to make sure I had my basic knot tying down, (Bowline, Water Knot, Figure Eight Double Knot, and Clove Hitch). Also, I thought about basic hydrology; know where both safety and danger lie. I was focused on the terminology of the river. River left, river right, up river, and down river is from the reference point of facing down river. These are terms I don't utilize daily but my confidence was high, and with Tyler and Mason on my team I knew we were well equipped.

We were getting closer to our designated location according to Google Maps. Tyler then switched to the Tact Channel, and hailed the Battalion Chief who was heading up the incident command. "Oceanside Lifeguards, go ahead, and pull up to the Rainbow Oaks Restaurant parking lot," he commanded. As we pulled in, we noticed all sorts of fire engines, ambulances, sheriff cars, and San Diego news media. The smell of barbecue permeated through the wet soggy air. There were people eating at this establishment while they watched the circus of first-responders all around them. *How can anyone eat while knowing there is a little boy downstream fighting for his life!* I thought.

With the exception of three firefighters in dry suits, the rest of them were walking around in boots and turnouts. They seemed surprised to see ocean lifeguards, but didn't pay us much mind. "If these firefighters aren't careful, they will be the next victim,"

Mason mumbled. Mason and I stayed by the truck as Tyler met with the Incident Command Chief. "We are the only ones here with a boat," Mason said. "Yeah, it's all going to fall on our laps before it's said and done," I added. "Ok, we're going to meet up with some Fallbrook firefighters about a half mile down creek," Tyler said. As we pulled out of the parking lot it dawned on me; *Where were the emotional parents? Where is the mom that should be running up and down the creek screaming for her little boy, or the dad being held back by first responders, demanding that he be allowed to jump into the creek to swim, and find his boy? It just didn't make sense.*

We rendezvoused to our designated search spot with the firefighters. We all met standing in the middle of a flooded street that the creek overflowed into. We looked around to make sure there were no whirlpools. When there is so much flooding, man-hole covers on the streets can get popped off. If the water starts to recede suddenly, you basically get one big toilet bowl. If the water is deep enough, potentially everything in the vicinity of the vortex will be flushed into the sewer. People have been known to drown because of this. Luckily, we didn't see any of this at the time.

After making introductions and small talk with the firefighters, we all made sure we had flashlights and throw-bags. We squeezed through the gate of a chain linked fence, and walked down the muddy road of a nursery. There were lines of palm trees everywhere in big wooden planters. 50 yards in we decided to go left in between two rows, and walk towards the swollen creek. It was tough getting down to the water. The bank was steep with wild, dense and thick vegetation. After each step we took our boots stuck in the sticky saturated river mud. We all held on to the person in front of us, just in case we slipped. The water was condensed into a little gully shooting out like a fire hose over boulders, trees, and bushes. There were strainers everywhere. It was hard to make out figures in the water because of the darkness. Every piece of paper, garbage bag, and countless amounts of other debris was potentially the boy we were looking for. After searching for approximately forty five minutes, we were summoned back to the parking lot for a body that had just been discovered in the water, up stream.

Upon arriving, we were informed that it was an older male they found on the other side of the creek, wedged into a small tree. He had been submerged by the raging water. To get to the creek we had to walk behind the restaurant, and pass some seedy looking one story motel rooms. It smelled like sewage from the over-flowing septic tank leaking all over the bank of the creek. The occupants had that typical wild eyed, extended lower jaw "look" associated with tweekers. They were pacing around nervously with all the commotion around them. Most of them were smoking cigarettes, and drinking soda as we passed by. Once we made it to the creek bed, we walked up stream about twenty yards. There were a couple of firefighters pointing to the opposite side of the creek. "Where's the body?" I asked. "Look at the submerged log and the bush just to the right of that. He is in the middle of those branches just barely above the surface," One of them informed me. It took me a few seconds to focus on the spot and then it jumped out at me. Holy shit! That's a body alright! The white male appeared to be around 60 years old with gray hair. His color didn't seem real. I mean, he was white as white paper! *He has been there for a while,* I thought. The clothes had been stripped off of him by the fierce rushing water. *What is he doing in there? Did he drown trying to rescue the little boy?*

The Fire Chief wanted to know if we could get him out. Tyler told him we would have to find some good anchor points if we were going to be rigging up any mechanical system. The three of us explored upstream to check out the lay of the land. There were no big sturdy trees, boulders, or manmade objects to anchor off of. We couldn't get any vehicle down to the creek bank because of the overgrowth and swampy environment. The property sixty yards up creek belonged to some eccentric wood carver. There were tikis, totem poles, and wooden sculptures everywhere. Also, there were miscellaneous tools, broken down cars, and agriculture equipment scattered all around us. The wooden shed resembled a floating house boat. Water was rushing below, and it looked as if it were going to wash away. *That is definitely something we need to be concerned about.*

Everything seemed to be against us. It was pitch dark, strainers everywhere, and even with upstream spotters there was too much debris floating down stream. *Is retrieving a body at this point really worth the risk?* I contemplated.

After 20 minutes of searching, thinking of a plan, we met with the three firefighters who were in dry suits. They were now part of our wet team. This meant all six of us were the only ones who would be going next to or in the water. This was called, "The Hot Zone." Firefighters and other rescue personnel were designated for the warm or cool zones. The "warm zone" is from the waterline to 10 feet back, and you must be wearing a PFD. If not, you are designated as the "cold zone." "Cold zone" is where the equipment is located, and dropped from trucks, or retrieved as needed; then transferred to the "warm zone."

The three firefighters were looking around full of **worry** knowing that this was not their environment. Even though we lifeguards are the most comfortable around water, it was even too dangerous for us. We will do our best to save the savable, but we are not going to risk our own lives for just a recovery. This person is deceased.

Tyler met up with the Fire Chief, and explained regrettably that it was too dangerous to put anyone in the water. Tyler desperately wanted to find the missing boy, but he also has a responsibility for the safety of his crew. This tugged at his heartstrings being a father, but he knew this was the right call. The Chief gave Tyler an understanding look, and sighed. The Sheriff Captain standing next to him volunteered one of his deputies to stand watch that night. "Would you guys be willing to come back early in the morning, help us retrieve the body and search for the boy?" Tyler told him if he goes through the channels, and talks to the Oceanside Chief, then he would be here at first light. He also added that the water needed to recede first, and that he will bring in the most experienced people.

As the three of us walked back to the truck we felt deflated. Not only could we not get the body out of the creek, but we had to call off the search for the little boy until morning. This was one of the hardest experiences of my life! Of all the years of my lifeguarding career, we have never called off a rescue. It went against everything I had ever been trained to do in my 30 years. As painful as it was, I had to remember this was a "swift water" rescue, and the rules play out differently.

I looked back full of *sorrow*, towards the place he was last seen screaming for his young life. *He must be so scared out there.* I thought. I could only hope that by a miracle someone would find the little guy alive when daybreak arrived, and the search could end. We all loaded ourselves into the lifeguard truck, and headed back to headquarters. Not one of us spoke a word to each other the whole ride back. This tested our *faith.*

The next day was Monday. I was back in the classroom teaching. I couldn't get my mind off the boy. Did they find the little guy? I should have arranged for a sub because my heart wasn't here. My heart was at the creek. I took several breaks, stepping outside of my classroom calling HQ for any updates. On one of my call ins, they told me that six of our most experienced swift water rescue lifeguards were sent out to help in the recovery of the man's body. They informed me, the water had receded significantly, and they were still searching for the boy. They also noticed a car that could not be seen the night before was right underneath the man. *What the hell? Did this guy try to cross the raging water with the boy inside the car with him last night?* My thoughts were very unsettling.

As I was desperately seeking information, Mason was on scene being put into the inflatable boat that had three lines attached to it. Two on each side of the back, and one connected to the middle of the bow. Because of his strength to size ratio, Mason was usually picked to crew this along with a heavier man to stabilize them from the back. Each line had a couple of men to pull or release tension to control the direction of the boat. One of the back lines was being controlled on the other side of the creek. Mason maneuvered himself behind the body as he leaned over the bow. With his arms wrapping around the victims chest from underneath his armpits Mason squeezes while leaning back. Mason struggled. The body was wedged in good. It slowly released as Mason tightened his grip, and pulled once more with everything he had. The body was bloated, heavy, and now half-way up over the bow. Sensing his grip was slipping, and the boat getting unsteady from the sudden shift of weight Mason yelled "Now... Pull!" Mason now barely hanging on, and the body slithering deeper into the water. Mason abandoned the idea of getting him all the way in the boat. He wasn't going to give up this battle! He held on like a vice as he frantically muscled them toward shore. The two teams on river right pulled in the boat as quickly as they could. Within a minute, the crew on shore had grabbed the dead man, and placed him in a waiting stokes basket onto the muddy bank. The warm team carried him up the incident command. There the body was prepared for the Coroner.

The next few days different search teams scoured the Rainbow Creek looking for the boy. The water level was a mere trickle a couple days later. They were able to walk right down to the creek bed. After five days of searching, the missing five year old was found not far from the nursery we initially checked. He was found with the help of specially trained cadaver dogs. He was buried in mud under heavy brush not visible above ground. This indicated that he was pinned in a strainer.

The Sheriff Department did a thorough investigation, and discovered that the missing boy was in the vehicle with this man. He was a friend of the grandma, whom, the boy lived with. Apparently, both of his parents were incarcerated. Nobody knows why they were out driving in those conditions that night or why he attempted to cross a road flooded by a creek. There was a lot of speculation, but nobody knows for sure.

This was crushing to everybody in the community, and this incident took a heavy toll on all of us who were part of the search. He was an innocent pre-schooler who was just beginning his young life. He didn't have a chance that night. No chance at all...

CHAPTER 17

JETTY EDDY

"God does not look you over for medals, degrees, or diplomas, but for scars!" ~ Elbert Hubbard

The jerky stop-and-go driving of my young partner behind the wheel of the lifeguard truck was bugging the crap out of me. I was trying to be patient. David Wilson was the newest EMT on staff, and had just gone through an emergency vehicle operation course (EVOC). So here he was, practicing with me as passenger. *Although, overly cautious and skittish, at least he's being safe,* I told myself. It was another beautiful Southern California day, so I just rolled down the window, and gazed out at the ocean. The summer breeze blew through the cab, accompanied by the sounds of crashing waves and children playing on the beach.

Besides our first names, my young friend and I had one other thing in common: we had both graduated from California State University at Chico, although I had done this 20 years earlier than him. Our conversation revolved around the changes and growth at the college, and in the city of Chico. We bantered about our favorite bars, places to hang out, as well as where we had lived. I couldn't help but think Chico had been way better in the 1980's, and early '90's. Nowadays, it just didn't seem as quaint and magical as it had once been. Just like everywhere, I thought, it has become crowded, and restricted by more rules and regulations. *Maybe it was just this day and age that bothered me,* I continued to muse. Most people seemed kind of shallow, self-absorbed, and politically correct.

My reminiscences and deep pondering were interrupted when a call came over the radio that a WaveRunner had run into the north jetty. The vessel was reported to be lodged in a part of it that runs perpendicular to the rest of the jetty, and faces west. We call this section of the jetty the "Devils Triangle" because waves crash directly on it, resulting in a deadly threat to boats, WaveRunners, swimmers, and surfers.

As we arrived at the jetty, I had Wilson grab his can and fins to recon the situation. Since he was a wiry former member of Chico's triathlon club, I knew he would get there fast. He took off effortlessly leaping gracefully over the rocks like a gazelle. I grabbed my handheld communications radio, and walked towards the end of the jetty. I figured the driver had probably panicked when he or she realized they were going to be smashed up against the rocks, ditched their WaveRunner, and had swam to safety, or been picked up by another passing vessel. I was waiting for Wilson to hold both arms up over his head in an "O" shape to signal everything was okay, or Code 4 (no assistance needed). It surprised me when instead, he yelled, "Call for more help!"

Looking towards the triangle, I noticed four-to-five-foot waves breaking right on top of it. Wilson started waving quickly overhead, motioning me to step on it, and get out there. Immediately, I picked up my pace, and arrived to see a male about 30 yards away from the WaveRunner wedged into the rocks.

It was easy to surmise what had happened. This guy must have ridden a swell right into the jetty, and then been thrown by the breaking waves. His body was jammed into a cavity way too small for his size. The only parts of him visible now were his upper torso and head. It had to have taken tremendous force to encase him like this. As far as rescuing him, there were two big problems; one of which was that he'd suffered head, neck, and back injuries, and was barely conscious. Secondly, waves were breaking right on top of him threatening to drown him. Saving him was going to be tough.

I should've grabbed our jetty bags out of the truck, I thought. These contained helmets, ropes, and gloves. As the senior lifeguard, I also felt it was my responsibility to keep my partner safe. A few years before this, two lifeguards had broken their backs basically making the same type of rescue. Safety was paramount! I called dispatch, and asked for more lifeguards to help extricate the victim.

Wilson made his way down to the man. He was holding him trying to protect his airway so that he could continue to breathe. Every time a wave broke, they would temporarily disappear from my sight inside the crashing curtain of water, returning to view once the water receded. The onslaught of waves was relentless. An Oceanside Harbor police officer made his way up onto the jetty after jumping off his patrol boat, and swimming in on the protected side. The officer was built like a linebacker, about 6'2" tall and 220 pounds. It instantly crossed my mind... *Great for lifting!* He quickly scrambled down the slippery, jagged rocks to assist my partner.

I stayed on top of the jetty continuing radio communication. I shouted to the two rescuers, "Hey guys! Don't try to get him out yet. We have help on the way!" The victim was a large man who weighed approximately 270 pounds. If they tried to get him out right away, it would have put them at risk of injury, and the victim at risk of even further injury. I wanted to go down there and help as soon as I could, instead of standing there agonizing over the situation. But, I was well aware that my job at that point was maintaining "comms", and being available as a rescue swimmer if anyone got hurt, and was then washed into the water.

An engine company arrived to our location, and I was all too happy to turn over comms to the fire captain. Right after that, I worked my way down to the action with a handful of other lifeguards who were now on the scene. I watched my footing carefully over very slippery rocks covered with razor-sharp barnacles. These pointy crustaceans had already taken their toll on Wilson and the police officer. I noticed red streaks of blood dripping down their arms, legs, and torsos. Wilson was getting thrown around like a rag-doll. A hundred pounds smaller than the victim, he was nonetheless risking his life to make sure the man didn't drown! What he lacked in size, he certainly made up for in heart and courage.

For the victim to be freed from the crevice he was squeezed into, he had to be lifted up and out. At this point, there were lifeguards on all levels of the jetty, with the fire crew on top. After careful maneuvering, we managed to loosen the victim from his prison of rocks, move him up towards the water, and then out. The waves had no mercy. Each time more were coming, we yelled warnings to each other of their menacing arrival. We clutched onto our victim, the rocks, and each other during the continual assault of water. We worked like a human chain, with all of us who were lifting the patient being braced by someone else so we wouldn't fall into the deep crevices ourselves. Finally, after 45 minutes of getting battered, we had our patient in a Stokes basket, ready to be walked the 200 yards to the beach.

The victim looked like a large piece of meat used by Rocky Balboa for boxing training. His body was purplish blue—basically one big bruise. His feet looked like those of a cadaver, not a living person. They were the color of white paper with chunks of flesh hanging off them. One of his legs had a deformed appearance from multiple breaks. The patient wasn't oriented due to being in shock, and the fire captain called for an air ambulance which would fly him to a hospital trauma unit.

After the victim had been loaded onto the helicopter, I noticed that everyone involved with the rescue was shredded and bruised from the rocks. Jokingly, I told Wilson that he looked like he'd slid down a cheese grater. He got a good chuckle out of that. Thankfully, though, we all managed to avoid being severely injured. We cleaned our wounds with fresh water and hydrogen peroxide; knowing how easily they could get infected because of the bacteria and other microorganisms associated with barnacles.

Wilson ended up getting the Medal of Valor for his willingness to go above and beyond the call of duty. At 21 years of age, with no medical insurance or benefits from full-time lifeguard status, he still didn't hesitate to put himself in harm's way to save another person's life. *Geez, the City of Oceanside is getting their money's worth*, I thought. In another of life's absurdities, here were these extremely brave people who made pennies compared to people in other city agencies. Being in a life-and-death situation with Wilson built, by far, more cohesion between him and I in an hour than our common alma mater. Having said this, I would still love to have a pitcher of Sierra Nevada with him at the Madison Bear Garden in downtown Chico...

The next day, I was at Tower 11, and saw one of the firefighters who had been at the rescue. Just out of the water after bodysurfing, he walked over to me, and the first thing out of his mouth was, "Dude, are you sore?" I responded, "I'm sore from my neck all the way down to the bottom of my feet." He nodded and said, "That was a lot of heavy lifting!" He was able to give me an update about the patient, who had sustained a lot of broken bones and internal injuries, but was expected to survive.

On September 25, 2017, David Wilson would be the first lifeguard in California to receive the State Medal of Valor.

Before 2015, the State of California did not recognize

lifeguards for this award. The City of Newport, Lifeguard Chief along with several others pushed for legislation to acknowledge lifeguards as a result of Ben Carlson's drowning while performing a rescue on July 6, 2014. He made the ultimate sacrifice giving his live for another.

***

My son, Cole, who was 14 years old at the time, asked if he could go to a bonfire with his best friends, Jack and Kameron, at the Oceanside harbor beach. I told him he could. It dawned on me as soon as he left that I should have warned him about playing on the north jetty near "The Devils Triangle." Even though Cole was young; he was a Junior Lifeguard, an avid surfer, and water polo player. He was also for the most part a very responsible kid for his age. Cole's brown hair, olive skin, green eyes, and tall swimmer's build is a chip off the old block! Many times, we are told he looks like the twins. The last thing he probably wanted was a lecture from his old man. However, I did question myself if I should call to remind him. *No, he knows better. He has been a Jr. Lifeguard for 6 summers and the instructors in JG's talk about how dangerous the "Devils Triangle" is all the time. They'll be fine.*

Cole's friend Jack was also 13 years old. However, he looked more the age of 17. A handsome, tall kid, standing 6' with bleach blonde hair, blue eyes, and a California tan. If given the chance to see him next to his parents, you would wonder where Jack got his height. His dad is 5'6", and his mom about 5'2" at best. Jack was adopted at birth in AZ, but he is a California guy through and through. He is a good kid, with a great heart, very respectful to adults, funny, and when an opportunity comes around, like many boys his age; he will try to push the envelope on any given situation. He attracts the girls with his boyish smile and fun-loving personality which makes him stand out in a crowd. Jack and Cole's brother-like bond started in middle school, became stronger in Jr. Lifeguards, and continues when surfing and playing water polo. They complement each other in a very good way.

Cole's friend, Kameron, is a long and lean 14 year old. His dad, mostly Cuban, and his mom 100 percent Polish with blonde hair and blue eyes. However, you will not find any blonde hair or blue eyes on Kameron. He took after his father. He looks like he has a year around tan with dark hair and brown eyes. He is a good looking boy, who has more energy than the average kid. He is the type that could go out with the boys, swim/hang at the beach all day, ride bikes home, and while the majority of the boys just want to chill out and relax, Kameron will be found doing the complete opposite. He will be the first in everyone's face asking, "What you guys want to do next?" He has endless amounts of energy and is enthusiastic and obviously outgoing! Cole and Kameron go back to elementary school, and they too have a brother-like bond. They fight like brothers, but at the end of the day they will have each other's back.

As the boys arrived at the beach late afternoon that day, they were ready for a night of fun! The 3 best friends quickly picked out a fire pit, organized their belongings around it, and waited for all their friends who were invited to show up. Cole, Jack and Kameron were especially excited on this evening because this was their first time hosting a beach bonfire without parents hovering. Girls would be showing up any minute too!

After a couple of hours going in and out of the surf, swimming and playing, the guys headed up to their fire pit. The group of young teenagers started to entertain the idea of taking a walk on the north jetty. The boys and girls were jumping over gaps between rocks, racing each other across the jetty like speed skaters. Laughing, talking, and carefree; they were all admiring the setting sun here at the cool place that they call home.

They decided to walk down near the end of the jetty where it splits off at a 45 degree angle. The fog horn at the junction sits on top of a cement support which is about 10 feet wide and 10 feet long. It sits up about 5 feet over the rest of the jetty. They decided to sit there, and watch the large surf slam against the rocks while being invigorated by the ocean spray as the sun set. They enjoyed the coolness of the water on this hot summer night.

Cole climbed halfway down the rocks, in between a set of large waves to test how slippery the rocks were. After realizing that they indeed were very slick he retreated back up the cement square to his awaiting friends. Kameron, not wanting to be out done by Cole, decided it would be funny to lay on a rock a little more than halfway down. Jack was experienced enough to know from his days of Jr. Lifeguards that the "Devil's Triangle" was nothing to be playing around with stayed up on the jetty. Kameron, wanting to show off for the girls, and not much of an experienced "beach boy" decided to test the incoming waves. He wanted to see if he could withstand the impact of the waves. The waves were at least seven foot. Some of the others were voicing their concerns to Kameron. Cole yelled, "Don't be stupid dude, you are going to get an ass whooping if you are not careful!" The rest of the group thought he was heading their warning, and on his way back up.

Kameron just ignored the warnings... Seconds before impact from a very large wave, Cole sits down a few feet above Kameron, and tries to grab his hand to get him out of harm's way. The wave exploded on the rocks in front of the two boys. Cole's hand slips from Kameron's, and he falls safely back against the jetty rocks. However, now Cole see's that Kameron has been tossed violently into and around the bottom of the jetty, and ends up sliding into a boulder with sharp barnacles. *No way! If another wave rolls in Kam's done!* When Cole got sight of him again, he could see the side of his face had been shredded by the sharp and razor-like edges of rock and barnacles. And, his earlobe was hanging by a thin strip of skin.

Cole knew he was the only one who could help his best friend, who was now in so much danger because Jack, unbeknownst to him didn't know Kameron had fallen in. "If I don't act quickly, this could be the death of both of us!" Cole thought. There was no time to summon up help. Cole knew he had to keep his composure, and proceeded with a plan on how to get Kameron out. He knew the worst thing that could happen is they both end up falling in. So, he watched the timing of the waves as they came in. He knew if he could get a break in the sets, he would have time to pull Kameron out. However, seven foot waves kept hammering down on them. Once he saw the water receding, Cole went for it! He reached for Kameron's hand again. He grabbed a hold of his hand, and screamed, "I got you Kam! Hang in their brother!" Cole knew there was no time for being scared. He just pulled on Kam's hand with every ounce of strength he had in him hoping his timing would beat the next large set of waves. As they struggled up the slippery rocks together, Cole couldn't believe what he was looking at. Kam's face was bleeding profusely and endlessly. He looked like the guys in war movies, but Cole knew this was no movie. He knew his buddy was in need of serious medical attention, and fast!

Cole yelled for Jack and the gang to help assist him the rest of the way up the rocks. Then, they proceeded to evaluate him. The bleeding just wouldn't stop. Cole threw one of his shirts to Mara, a Jr. Lifeguard herself. She began tending to Kameron's wounds. Because of his repetitive questions, the kids who are Jr. Lifeguards suspected the Kameron had a concussion. "Where is my favorite hat?" Over and over again he kept asking. As a group, they assisted him back to the fire pit. Jack and another boy knew that he needed help as soon as possible, and decided to run to lifeguard headquarters about a mile away. Cole and Mara had taken charge of the situation; both decided not to call 911. They felt that if they did his parents would get slammed with a very expensive ambulance bill. All the kids learned a very important lesson about that. No matter what, you ALWAYS call 911!

Jack and his buddy made the mile run to headquarters as fast as they could. It was now past 8 pm, and the last lifeguards where getting off duty. Jack saw a young man getting into his car, and yelled to him. He knew he was a lifeguard even though he didn't look more than 18 years old. They told him that their friend was injured, and needed help at the harbor. "We are all off duty. Get into my truck, and we will drive up there", he said. Relieved, the boys climbed in, and told the lifeguard in more detail what had happened, and the degree of the injuries as they knew them. When they arrived to the fire pit near Tower 16, the lifeguard ran up the tower steps and opened it up. He grabbed the first aid kit, and then assessed the injuries. All kids assisted the lifeguard in bandaging up Kameron. They kept talking to him, and tried to stay calm while Cole made the painful and horrifying call to his parents.

Kameron's parents were enjoying dinner as the phone rang. "Yes Kam," his mom answered. "No, it's Cole," he said. She gasped, and asked what was wrong? After hearing what happened they quickly paid the bill, and jetted to the scene. As they arrived, Kameron's dad, Mark, thanked the lifeguard as he got Kam into the vehicle. Sylvia, thanked Cole, Jack, and the other kids for helping Kameron. They were shocked seeing the injuries – even though he had been bandaged up. Off they went to the hospital. It ended up being a long night for their family. Kameron had his earlobe sewn back on, his jaw wired shut as a result of a broken jawbone, and many, many stitches to the face. The doctors also felt he was mildly concussed. Kameron has since healed from all the injuries. However, the lessons learned will be with him, and all of the teenagers for a lifetime.

We all know the old adage, this could have been way worse. This has strengthened my son Cole's resolve to become a lifeguard one day. Just like his grandfather, uncles and I did. He has caught the fever, and now has dedicated himself to achieving this goal that runs so deep in his family blood… Lifeguard Blood! As his father, I could not be more proud, and humbled knowing my son wants to carry on the family tradition of being a waterman.

CHAPTER 18

FINAL REFLECTIONS

"A ship is always safe at the shore, but that is not what it is built for." ~ Albert Einstein

Growing up, I really hated swimming. Out of four brothers, I was the slowest, probably because I despised it the most. Every day, we would ride our bikes down to the pool, jump into the cold water, and chase the black line for two hours. My friends seemed far luckier—they played baseball, a game with friends who chewed sunflower seeds, and drank soda in the dugout. Plus, they wore cool uniforms and hats, while we shivered away in our Speedo's. We battled against ourselves, the running clock, and trying to make the interval dreamt up by some psychotic coach.

Obviously, swimming is good for you. I can't think of another exercise more effective in developing muscle strength, endurance, and cardiovascular fitness. Just like running, it can put you in a meditative state when done over prolonged distances.

There is also a strong psychological benefit to swimming. As a teacher, when I look around at the students who are athletes, swimmers are the fittest. Swim workouts are a grind with an intensity fueled by the pressure to keep up with the pack, and survive. However, they serve as training in dealing with pain, building persistence, and developing a mental toughness which transfers over into the rest of life.

So, thank you to my parents for making me and my siblings swim. We may not be professional athletes, but we can go anywhere in the world, and get paid to lifeguard. As a parent, I think teaching your child to swim is an essential form of "tough love." Teaching a youngster to swim is not for the faint of heart. There might be a lot of crying and screaming, but you must work through it. I recommend not having other parents or relatives around, because they may judge the process as abusive, without understanding how important it is… possibly even the difference between life and death one day.

At the risk of sounding sappy; teaching a child to swim is also a time of bonding between you and your child. The swimming pool can seem like a big, scary place to a kid. When jumping in, they are taking a risk, and putting their complete trust in you. Their lives are literally in your hands. When they go underwater for the first time, and look into your eyes while you are at the bottom of the pool with them, it's a truly magical moment. They will never forget this experience, or the intimate relationship it cemented with you. At some point, they will appreciate the fact that you put the time and energy into teaching them not just to swim, but a more important life lesson: to take chances, and test themselves.

Learning to swim can be compared to the different stages of life, some of which feel like jumping into a pool for the first time. But in order to evolve, we have to take calculated risks, and work hard. As intimidating as this can seem, I think everyone should go outside their comfort zone now and then for the sake of personal development. As one of my favorite historical figures of all times, General George S. Patton, put it, "Accept challenges, so that you may feel the exhilaration of victory."

* * *

"Experience is a jewel, and it had need be so, for it is often purchased at an infinite price." ~ William Shakespeare

Being a lifeguard for nearly 30 years, like living itself, has been filled with juxtaposing positive and negative, comedy and tragedy, euphoria and heartbreak. All the knowledge I've gained during these years about rescue operations, surf conditions, and even other people, still does not compare to what I've learned about myself. My experiences have had a huge role in making me who I am now. Here are a few items, both observational and philosophical, which come to mind when I consider my lifeguarding "education":

- Beginning is the hardest step.

- No matter how tough things are going, don't quit.

- Competition makes you better.

- Be inspired, and do your best to be an inspiration to others.

- Whenever there is a trauma on the beach, there is almost always a know-it-all firefighter in the crowd—who wants everyone to *know* he is a firefighter. This individual will proceed to tell everyone where they should be standing, what they should be doing, and at the end of the scene, remind all present that he is, indeed, a firefighter.

- There is also an individual in every crowd who can spiritually connect with animals. If we are trying to assist or rescue an animal, such as a sea lion, these people seem to come out of the woodwork to tell you that you are scaring it or that you're putting off a "bad vibe."

- For some reason, people love digging holes in the sand—and not just any hole, but huge, deep holes. They will show up at the beach with shovels and dig all day. Unfortunately, people get buried alive in these holes, which is becoming an increasingly frequent emergency situation. In the last ten years, there have been two near-fatal incidents related to hole-digging on the beaches I patrol. One young boy was buried, and unconscious by the time he was dug out. To this day, he has breathing problems because of the fine sand particles he breathed into his lungs.

- Most people will stop everything that they are doing to help the lifeguards look for missing kids.

- Fire pits or lack of them are the most common cause of arguments on the beach.

- People who come to the beach by themselves, and sit on the rocks, staring out at the ocean, are dealing with personal issues.

- All guys throwing footballs on the beach think they are pro quarterbacks just waiting to be discovered.

- You can't save everybody.

- The beach attracts a lot of very interesting people. It's worthwhile to spend a few minutes each day to talk to at least one of them.

- There are certain people whom I see *every day* at the beach. Don't they work?

- Some people want a specific water temperature every day, and become quite upset if the water doesn't cooperate.

- People who are in tune with the ocean seem to be very well-rounded individuals.

- The ocean can humble you.

- When getting pounded by big surf, and being held underwater… relax your breathing, and start counting calmly. Rarely will you reach "15" before you resurface.

- It is profoundly fulfilling to look after others, and put them before yourself.

The Wagner Family. The Oceanside Pier, 1987

Back row: Bill and Ruth
Middle row: Scott, Lori and Mike
Front row: Neal and David

Bonanza: Wagner style!

Left to right: Neal, Mike, Brother-in-law Darren, Bill, David and Scott

Summer of Young Love 1996

70's/80's Theme Lifeguard Party
Jennifer and David

Family day at "The Office!"

Left to right: Brianna, Jennifer, David and Cole

Medal of Valor, 2015

Oceanside Lifeguard Recipients:
David Wagner, Nathan Parker and Ryan Thompson

Best Bro's!

Kameron, Jack & Cole, 2018

ABOUT THE AUTHOR

David Wagner has lived in Oceanside, California all his life. Raised in a large family where swimming was like breathing, and working hard was the *only* option, Dave got an early start learning the skills he'd need for what would later become over three decades of surf beach lifeguarding. By successfully applying the same basic values from his childhood to all areas of his life, he earned his B.A. from California State University, Chico, continued to work lifeguarding and training Junior Lifeguards for several summers. On the way, Dave discovered he has a knack for teaching; leading him to his current position as history teacher at Oceanside High School, where he also coached the school's swim and water polo teams.

In his free time, Dave enjoys surfing, friendly competition playing basketball and ultimate Frisbee. His drive, passion, and dedication find their greatest outlet, however, in his wife and two children, without whose love and support this book would not have come to be.

Made in the USA
San Bernardino, CA
12 April 2018